Catch *the* Ball

Get in the Game!
A Devotional for the Alpha Male

Rev. Charles A. Bledsoe

WestBow
PRESS®
A DIVISION OF THOMAS NELSON
& ZONDERVAN

Copyright © 2019 Rev. Charles A. Bledsoe.

All rights reserved. No part of this book may be used or reproduced by any means, graphic, electronic, or mechanical, including photocopying, recording, taping or by any information storage retrieval system without the written permission of the author except in the case of brief quotations embodied in critical articles and reviews.

This book is a work of non-fiction. Unless otherwise noted, the author and the publisher make no explicit guarantees as to the accuracy of the information contained in this book and in some cases, names of people and places have been altered to protect their privacy.

THE HOLY BIBLE, NEW INTERNATIONAL VERSION®,
NIV® Copyright © 1973, 1978, 1984, 2011 by Biblica, Inc.®
Used by permission. All rights reserved worldwide.

WestBow Press books may be ordered through booksellers or by contacting:

WestBow Press
A Division of Thomas Nelson & Zondervan
1663 Liberty Drive
Bloomington, IN 47403
www.westbowpress.com
1 (866) 928-1240

Because of the dynamic nature of the Internet, any web addresses or links contained in this book may have changed since publication and may no longer be valid. The views expressed in this work are solely those of the author and do not necessarily reflect the views of the publisher, and the publisher hereby disclaims any responsibility for them.

Any people depicted in stock imagery provided by Getty Images are models, and such images are being used for illustrative purposes only.
Certain stock imagery © Getty Images.

ISBN: 978-1-9736-4559-7 (sc)
ISBN: 978-1-9736-4558-0 (hc)
ISBN: 978-1-9736-4560-3 (e)

Library of Congress Control Number: 2018913495

Print information available on the last page.

WestBow Press rev. date: 03/18/2019

The book dedicated to my wife and best
friend, Susan L. (Crump) Bledsoe.

She stands beside me; supports, counsels, and encourages
me; reprimands, disciplines, and (according to my
mother) raises me up to become the man I am today.

Who knew our meeting on the girls softball field
in Point Pleasant, West Virginia, fifty-two years ago
would turn into a lifetime in ministry together.

Contents

Preface ix

Introduction xi

The Alpha Male's Ultimate Challenge

    "Offer your bodies as living sacrifices" 1

First Principle

    "Do not conform any longer to the pattern of this world" 15

Second Principle

    "Do not think of yourself more highly than you ought" 31

Third Principle

    "Love must be sincere" 55

Preface

Catch the Ball—Get in the Game intends to challenge you and make you think—a lost art in our society. I know men who are reluctant to speak up in a group with women present. Churches are usually comprised of over 60 percent women, creating an issue for many men. Men must not remain silent, especially in our churches.

The screaming silence of men at church is punctuated by the lack of masculine participation in ministry. It's the church's version of taxation without representation. Unintentionally, many churches want male participation without providing a masculine oriented listening ear, or responsive leadership. Men need masculine teaching and preaching to encourage them to get in the game.

Men desire a church (and devotional material) that values and respects their masculine souls. Alpha Males hunger for worship experiences addressing their unidentified cravings for challenge, risk, danger, and doing the impossible, all for the glory of God.

Because of this, *Catch the Ball* is more direct than some devotionals. Alpha Males prefer straight-up truth without fluff, butterflies, and kittens. Instead they want it direct and in your face. I trust your masculine soul can handle it.

Thank you for purchasing *Catch the Ball—Get in the Game*. I am grateful for your willingness to take a risk and buy this book. Help me improve by e-mailing your questions, insights, and observations to:

CatchTheBall121@gmail.com

Blessings on you!
Rev. Charles A. Bledsoe

Introduction

What is an Alpha Male?

He's not what you think!

When we think of Alpha Males, we think of the kingly lion, the stealth alligator, the sleek killer whale, or the deadly bull shark. Our mind goes to the most feared predator list, and rightly so.

We also think of Hollywood creations like Rambo, James Bond, xXx (Xander Cage), and Captain America. Fearless men, who are never defeated in hand-to-hand combat, are expert marksmen, and who always gets the beautiful girl in the end. You know the type. No, I can't identify with them either.

Dr. Robert Lewis, author of *Quest for Authentic Manhood*, offers a biblical definition for a biblical man (Alpha Male) with whom I can identify. He:

- Rejects passivity
- Accepts responsibility
- Acts courageously
- Waits for the reward only God gives

I recommend you review his challenging "33 The Series" Bible study.

www.authenticmanhood.com

Being an Alpha Male has nothing to do with:

- Muscle size, fitness level, or combat skills
- Education, income, or vocation
- Looks, personality, or ability to attract women
- Height, weight, body piercings, or tattoos

- Car, truck, motorcycle, boat, or ATV
- Skill level in sports
- Clothes or electronic gadgets

Many men believe what they do transforms the inward man. They hope the things they own and the exaggerations they speak fill the voids in their souls and eradicate their haunting deficiencies. Deficiencies they hope no one sees, but many do. For many men, the phase "Let the games begin!" is a non-fulfilling, empty lifestyle of game-playing hopelessness, loneliness, and self-doubt. The Bible is full of examples of men who look successful and manly but are actually empty, unfulfilled, and weak on the inside, where the real man abides. Samson is a very good, bad-example.

Question: Do sharp claws and teeth make the large cat a lion, or does the beast inside make the large cat with sharp claws and teeth a lion?

As a boy, I heard,

> "It's not the size of the dog in the fight.
> It's the size of the fight in the dog."

Our journey to Alpha Manhood is difficult so few take it. Many want the easy route so they accept the world's definition of an Alpha Man and build a façade, concealing their true identity. They take the wrong trail, the external trail.

The internal trail to true Alpha Manhood is revealed in Scripture. Only men who deeply desire Alpha Manhood take this journey. As in mountain climbing, only those who possess the do-or-die mentality reach the summit. They discover the reward is greater than their dreams, and they gain benefits that cannot be fully expressed in earthly language

Following God's leadership is difficult. It means you must say, pray, and live "Not my will, but yours be done!" For men, yielding our will to another runs against our DNA to make the decision, set the course, and lead the charge. As we enthrone Christ in our lives, we acknowledge His Kingship and voluntarily bend our will beneath

His. We truly recognize our Father knows best. Then we do the manly thing: we follow His leadership, travel the course He sets, and charge life with the power of His Holy Spirit living in us.

Make no mistake: bending our will beneath His will is the front line in our spiritual war. It's where Satan strongly confronts us with our worldly manhood, telling us it is our life so we must maintain complete control and call the shots. The fiercest battles are fought every time we must bend our will beneath God's will once again.

Every man can succeed if he becomes more determined to win the internal battle. In the TV reality show *Biggest Loser*, many contestants act the same. They whine, complain, lie, cheat, connive, take the "poor me" attitude, and declare they are "going to die" unless they can find an easier way to their goals. They quit early and make excuses. The truth is they did not follow their diet or workout plans. They choose the easy road to failure instead of the harder road to success.

They whine, declare themselves victims, make excuses, and quit early—an all too familiar tune.

Compare that type of person to those who focus their vision, work harder, endure the pain, persevere with intense determination, follow the plan, and finish the challenge. When done, they collapse. Everything is expended and nothing is left. They run the race set before them and finish the course! These are champions even if they do not become the *Biggest Loser*.

> How determined are you to focus your vision,
> work harder, endure the pain, and persevere as God enables
> you to finish the transformation course set before you?

We cannot complete this journey, our calling, using our personal, human strengths. We need the Holy Spirit in our lives to make us more than conquerors. We do not fight against flesh and blood but powers and principalities. The time we spend reading His Word, talking with Him, worshipping Him, and serving Him is time invested in becoming what God calls us to become. The key is not doing. *The key is becoming.*

Men need each other more than we care to realize or admit. We've been loners so long we are uncomfortable around other men. We even believe we do not need anyone except our families, and sometimes not even them. We think our aloneness is a positive character quality even though strong, credible research says otherwise.

I strongly encourage you to find a man, or team, to take this journey with you. Find someone to encourage you and whom you can encourage as you both intentionally grow in your walk with Jesus Christ.

King Solomon wrote in Proverbs 27:17,

"As iron sharpens iron, so one person [Alpha Man] sharpens another."

Accept this as absolute truth.
Believe this with as much faith as you can muster!
Live it in the power of the indwelling Holy Spirit!
Who will you ask to join you on your Alpha Man journey?

It's your time!

Your time to begin is now!

Your place to begin is here!

- If not you, Who?
- If not now, When?
- If not here, Where?

Side Note: My three-year-old, thirty-eight inch tall, thirty pound grandson is an Alpha Male. I know this because when Ethan pretends to be a jungle animal, he is a tiger or lion. When pretending to be a superhero, he's the Incredible Hulk. He's also a T-Rex, a policeman or a fireman. Ethan instinctively chooses to be on top of the food chain!

No butterflies, hummingbirds, puppies, or soft and fuzzy things for him. Even with his kind and tender heart, he is powerful and strong.

Edification Exercise: Define power.
                        Define strength.
                        How are they alike?
                        How are they different?

Why would I tame Ethan's Alpha Man spirit? When God gives you an Alpha Man vision, do you want to approach it with the heart of Pee-Wee Herman or Arnold Schwarzenegger?

Every man to ever walk this earth is endowed by the Creator with Alpha Male DNA. It is my responsibility to cultivate the powerful Alpha Man in Ethan so no one crushes his God-given potential and purpose. What is your responsibility to yourself and the Alpha Male wanna-be's in your life?

I want to hear from you! Please e-mail your thoughts, insights, and observations to me at:

CatchTheBall121@gmail.com

Semper Fi, Brothers

THE ALPHA MALE'S ULTIMATE CHALLENGE

> Therefore,
> I urge you, bothers,
> in view of God's mercy,
> to offer your bodies as living sacrifices,
> holy and pleasing to God—
> this is your spiritual act of worship.
> —Romans 12:1

1

"Therefore ..." (Romans 12:1)

Have you ever wondered, "If I made different choices, what would my life be like today?" Some examples are "What if I had ..."

- Taken high school more seriously
- Heeded the advice of elders with a long view of life
- Went to college instead of [complete this phrase]
- Not partied so hard in high school or college
- Bought 3,000 shares of Delphi stock in 2009 at 33 cents per share, then sold it in 2018 at $84.33 a share
- Teamed up with God much earlier in my life
- Taken my faith more seriously
- Followed God's leadership more faithfully and obediently

By writing "Therefore," Paul reveals faith builds our lives. The decisions we make, one stacked upon the next, bring us to where we are today and take us where we will be in the future. The quality of our faith-based choices is critical. The question is not "Will we build?" but "What will we build?" Just like in construction, building material quality determines the quality of the building.

"Therefore" embraces the past, engages the present, and excitingly anticipates a better future. "Therefore" says we must use the building materials previously written and continue our build using truth about to be written. It is time for us to build our legacy and bless future generations with lives worthy of the calling of Christ.

As you remodel your house, you know the process is painful, stressful, uncomfortable, and inconvenient, requiring dedication and persistence. The same is true with your transformation. It is painful, stressful, uncomfortable, and inconvenient, requiring dedication and persistence, but it ends with amazing results. Self-discipline today paves the way to greater victories tomorrow!

Your past is carved in stone and cannot be changed. However, your future is still untouched. Your age or life situation does not matter. The only important question is, "Am I willing to make biblical decisions today to improve the quality of my life both now and in the future?"

The Point: "The only pain greater than the pain of self-discipline is the pain of regret." (Dr. John C. Maxwell)

- Describe the pains of regret you have experienced.
- What self-discipline pains are you experiencing now?
- List one self-discipline delivering positive, present-day results in your life.
- How is your life better than it was five, ten, or twenty-five years ago?
- How is your life building the legacy you want and your family deserves?

Remember thinking, "If I knew back then what I know now"? Thanks to Paul's "Therefore," you now know the way to a better future as you look forward to a renewed understanding of Romans 12 with exciting anticipation!

2

"Therefore, I urge you, brothers…"
(Romans 12:1)

My parents taught me begging is not good manners, and neither does it help build a quality reputation. Begging is an undesirable characteristic to avoid.

Some say Paul was begging the Romans Christians to listen and apply what he was teaching to their lives. I cannot read, write, or speak Greek, and so I must not argue their "begging" point. However, I will share my interpretation.

Paul was not speaking like a street beggar to a mark, but like a wise sibling to an inexperienced or unwise brother. Let me explain. A beggar targets someone and tells his sad story, hoping to stir their emotions so they will give him a few coins. To the beggar, it is all about himself, his needs, his wants, and his situation.

The wise sibling approaches a brother with wisdom and insight, offering an opportunity to see the long view of where his decisions will take him. To the wise sibling it is all about his brother's security, safety, and future.

The beggar uses manipulation to get us to do something for his benefit.

The wise sibling uses insight and inspiration to motivate a bother to do something for his brother's benefit.

> Paul is your wise brother, who has your best
> interests at the center of his heart!

King David wanted to make a burnt offering to God, and so Araunah offered David all the items needed—for free. King David replied,

> "No, I insist on paying you for it. I will not sacrifice to the Lord my God burnt offerings *that cost me nothing*" (2 Samuel 24:24).

Read the entire 24th chapter to understand the powerful context surrounding this verse.

Our salvation is provided by Jesus Christ on Calvary. Our spiritual growth is not free but requires sacrifice to develop the disciplines needed for our journey. Society teaches us to sacrifice nothing. However if we give anything it must not cost us anything.

The journey to becoming an Alpha Male is not easy and requires a personal investment. Only the determined who hunger for their Lord will discover victory.

The Point: God is not trying to manipulate you to do something for Him. God inspires and motivates you with truth for a powerful, hope-filled present and future life.

- What can you do to implement your brother's wise leadership to see the long view of your life?
- How much will you adjust your course so you aim for the painful, challenging, and best instead of the comfortable, slothful, and easy?
- What is so valuable you are not willing to sacrifice it to the Lord?

3

"Therefore, I urge you, brothers, in view of God's mercy ..." (Romans 12:1)

Mercy: You do NOT receive what you deserve.

Grace: You receive what you do NOT deserve.

Mercy: Why God did not terminate your life because of your sin.

Grace: Why God sent Jesus to die for your sins so you may receive forgiveness and eternal life.

Grace and Mercy, Siamese twins, born in the heart of our holy God. coexisting exclusively for our total benefit. King David explores the seemingly unreasonable, selfless love of God when he writes,

> "What is man that You are mindful of him, the son of man that You care for him?" (Psalm 8:4)

Two good questions. Go ahead; attempt an answer!

Paul is urging us to walk through Roman "in view of God's mercy." God hungers for a relationship with us not because we deserve it, but because He knows our lives are best when we receive all He has to give. We need God, but He does not need us. God is the wise Father seeking to inspire and motivate us to become Spirit-filled, Spirit-led disciples of Christ.

In Ephesians 2:8–9, Paul emphasizes and clarifies this point.

> For it is by grace you have been saved, through faith—
> and this not from yourselves, it is the gift of God—not
> by works, so that no one can boast.

It's about what God does for us and not what we do for ourselves.

Only 10 percent of men follow the doctor's instructions to improve our health. Is this same percentage true concerning following God's instructions to improve the health of our spiritual lives?

Shakespeare said it well: "To be or not to be; that is the question."

The Point: The choice is either to be or not to be all that God desires for you. It's your choice—choose carefully and wisely.

- What choice can you make right now enabling you to be in the 10 percent?
- How would you explain this concept to a new brother in Christ?
- Explain the difference between "to be" and "to do."
- What are the results of doing what God requires?
- What are the results of becoming what God requires?
- How can you explain this to your teenage son?

4

"Therefore, I urge you, brothers, In view of God's mercy, to offer your bodies as living sacrifices ..." (Romans 12:1)

A video image burns within the theater of my imagination.

The wide receiver advanced five yards and then sharply turned toward the dangerous, well-guarded middle of the field. The quarterback fired a rocket a few feet above the receiver's head, and without hesitation he leaped into the air and snagged this perfectly placed football, quickly pulling it into his chest. While he was still in the air, a defensive back hit the receiver's feet, spinning his feet up in the air.

A split second later, the rock-hard, speeding Mack truck called a linebacker hit the receiver from the opposite direction, spinning the receiver almost completely around, causing him to land flat on his back in the middle of the field. The crowd silently held their breath until the referee's outstretched arm signaled, "First down!" Exuberant celebration exploded for a few moments. Then silence quickly filled the stadium. The receiver was not getting up.

Within seconds, the medical staff ran to the downed receiver. The ball was carefully pried from his clutches as they immobilized his neck and back. The cart quickly arrived, and they very carefully placed his unconscious body on it. Players from both benches hit their knees while other players and fans stood in circles, clearly praying for this injured player. Muffled cheers filled the air as he was driven off the field because everyone realized this man may have life-threatening injuries.

When I think about sacrifice, this image always rushes to the surface. The receiver's intention was not to be injured but to catch the ball for a first down. Even though the price he paid was higher than expected, he still caught the ball, making it possible for his team to score a touchdown a few plays later.

I have never witnessed a crucifixion. After viewing Mel Gibson's film *The Passion of Christ*, I'm still fuzzy on the details. Yet I am more aware of the cost God paid so I could join His team and win the game. The price Jesus paid far exceeds anything I can ever pay back in a thousand lifetimes.

Paul's challenge to "offer your bodies as living sacrifices" is not asking us to physically die for men who do not know Christ. God wants us to die to self! We should intentionally live a hope-filled life so men see our optimistic life and ask why we have hope when the world is in such a hopeless mess.

The Point: The clearest evidence of being a "living sacrifice disciple" is our determination to catch the ball thrown into very difficult situations. Here we fight the most fierce battles, take the greatest risks, and potentially pay the highest price.

- What will it take for you to catch the ball in dangerous situations?
- What preparations must you do to get ready for this type of catch?
- How does preparation change your life and lifestyle?
- Whom can you team up with so both can advance toward the goal?
- Will you catch the ball?

5

"Therefore, I urge you, brothers, in view of God's mercy, to offer your bodies as living sacrifices, holy and pleasing to God …" (Romans 12:1)

Some things are meant to be together: Peanut butter and jelly, ham and cheese, a man and a woman, father and son, torque and horsepower. Ah, yes, Mustangs and V8s! Some things belong together!

Holy and pleasing are two qualities that cannot be separated. These two terms qualify the only sacrifice God accepts.

Holy means sinless; pure; without defilement, defect, or flaw; mature; perfect in every way.

Webster's dictionary defines *pleasing* as: agreeable, blessed, congenial, delicious, good, heavenly, savory, welcome.

Is this possible? No, not by human strength. So how do I offer a holy and pleasing sacrifice to God?

It's a matter of motive. Your motive is the *why* behind the drive to do something. My wife's quickness to recognize my motive is revealed when she asks questions like, "Okay, what do you want?" or "What have you done now?" No matter how clever or pious we think we are, we cannot hide or disguise any motive from God.

God sent Samuel to the house of Jesse to anoint Israel's new king. When Samuel met Eliab (David's brother), he was so impressed by Eliab's physical appearance, God had to renew Samuel's thinking. Read the entire chapter, but this particular verse is worth noting.

But the LORD said to Samuel, "Do not consider his appearance or his height, for I have rejected him. The LORD does not look at the things people look at. People look at the outward appearance, but the LORD looks at the heart." (1 Samuel 16:7)

The Point: Your motives determine the quality of your sacrifice and the price you are willing to pay.

- How does "In view of God's mercy" enhance the definition of "holy and pleasing to God"?
- What does it mean to you to "offer your bodies as a living sacrifice"?
- How do our motives affect the quality of our sacrifice?
- How do our motives determine the price we are willing to pay?
- How can our motives be transformed so they are truly "holy and pleasing" to God?
- How would you explain this principle to a new believer?

6

"Therefore, I urge you, bothers, in view of God's mercy, to offer your bodies as living sacrifices, holy and pleasing to God – this is your spiritual act of worship." (Romans 12:1)

Susan, my wife, is a great cook who prefers cooking from scratch. She has not found a receipt that can escape her personal touch. During Thanksgiving and Christmas, she pulls out all the stops and throws herself into some serious baking. Her efforts make Thanksgiving and Christmas my favorite holidays!

I learn from observing Susan's baking skills in full action. The flour, sugar, baking soda, eggs, milk, and flavorings are common items that become a delicious, uncommon treat when mixed by her skillful hands.

That's what God wants: common men offering uncommon, delicious worship.

Worship has various expressions.

Corporate—men gather in a building, tent, cabin, or lean-to, or under a canopy of trees and sky, to collectively lift their hearts and voices to praise and honor God. They pray and study God's Word as a team in search of God's will for their collective lives.

Private—an individual man finds a place to lift his heart and voice in praise to his personal God; to pray and study God's Word in search of God's will for his life.

Worship means "to serve" making everything we do a spiritual act of worship.

Worship service suggests we gather to collectively praise and honor God.

Worship as service suggests our individual expression of faith is fleshed out by serving others. The ultimate purpose of worship as service is to introduce others to God's grace and mercy so they can experience His forgiveness and grace.

Worship service is us telling God how much we love Him.

Worship as service is us showing others how much God loves them.

Up to now, everything Paul wrote to the Romans leads us to one concept: what "offer your bodies as living sacrifices" looks like. The remaining chapters in Romans teach us how this offering is fleshed out in our lives and how it expresses itself in thought and action. The rest of this devotional is my attempt to share my understanding of what verse 1 looks like when we allow God to work through our lives.

The Point: Sunday's worship service is the launching pad for our daily "worship as service" lifestyle.

- What does your worship service look like to you?
- What does your "worship as service" look like to you?
- What must you become to flesh out these worship differences?
- How can you explain these differences to your daughter?

First Principle

Do not conform any longer to the pattern of the world. (Romans 12:2a)

COMMENTARY

"But be transformed by the renewing of your mind. Then you will be able to test and approve what God's will is—

His good, pleasing and perfect will. (Romans 12:2b)

Before We Begin the Next Section

We have a tendency to fulfill our spiritual duties like it's a honey-do list.

- ☑ Change light switch in bedroom
- ☑ Pray
- ☑ Caulk bathroom window
- ☑ Read the Bible
- ☑ Shampoo family room carpet
- ☑ Call Joe—missed church
- ☑ Trim hedges away from front sidewalk
- ☑ Call Bill—invite to ballgame
- ☑ Get water softener salt
- ☑ Do one good deed

Box checking is legalism, and Legalism is cannibalism of the Spirit. It:

- ✗ Consumes joy and leaves indifference
- ✗ Consumes pure motives and leaves cold, heartless lives.
- ✗ Consumes satisfaction and leaves emptiness
- ✗ Consumes energy and leaves weariness
- ✗ Consumes participation and leaves spectatorship
- ✗ Consumes love and leaves apathy
- ✗ Consumes passion and leaves antipathy
- ✗ Consumes life and leaves death

Are you simply checking boxes right now?

As you read these devotions, ask the Lord for understanding and strength to apply what you learn. James hit this point like a defensive tackle hits a quarterback when he wrote,

> Do not merely listen to the word, and so deceive yourselves. **Do what it says.** Anyone who listens to the word but does not do what it says is like a man who looks at this face in the mirror and, after looking at himself, goes away and immediately forgets what he looks like. But the man who looks intently into the perfect law that gives freedom, and continues to do this, not forgetting what he has heard, **but doing it**— he will be blessed in what he does." (James 1:26–27; emphasis added)

Serving God is embracing His lifestyle while allowing God to reprogram our minds, purify our motives, and modify our behaviors. Serving on God's team is transformational from the inside out.

By reprogramming our minds, God enables us to think like He thinks.

By purifying our motives, God empowers us to do the right thing for the right reason and at the right time.

By changing our behavior, God strengthens our actions so men who do not know God will read His Word and see His will at work in our lives.

Our behavior must not smear the Word or fog the view. I suggest seven major principles are presented in Romans 12:2–15:13, helping us implement our calling found in verse 1. The verses following each principle reveal how each looks when fleshed out. We cannot simply check the boxes and at the end lean back in our chairs and declare, "I have arrived!"

Reading God's Word does not mean we have experienced anything. It means we are exposed to God's transformational power. By reading a map, we have not taken a journey. However, it does mean we now know how to get to our desired destination if we take the journey.

I pray these truths challenge your mind and stir your masculine soul to seek God's indwelling Spirit, who purifies your heart and empowers you to become what He desires: "to act justly and to love mercy and to walk humbly with your God" (Micah 6:8).

I trust we discover the good news of Christ enhances and empowers our masculinity. Christ is the perfect Alpha Man: He rejects passivity, acts courageously, accepts responsibility, and waits for the reward only God can give. For Jesus, this means He chooses the best path for His life even though that path leads to Calvary.

Christ empowers our masculine spirit by the Holy Spirit's power, so we become Christian men serving God the way Christian men serve. Let us use our masculine souls, our masculine gifts, our masculine minds, and our masculine strengths to change our world for God's glory.

I trust we learn everything good in our lives is His doing and not our own. God transforms us so what we do is "holy and pleasing" because we cannot do either by ourselves.

Now, let's continue our journey as we prayerfully learn to walk the talk and become an Alpha Male! The first principle is waiting for you!

7

"Do not conform any longer ..." (Romans 12:2)

By visiting a local high school, you see teens determined to develop their clothing, behavior, or attitude styles. However, they are individuals in their minds only, not realizing they are conforming to the demands of their culture or subculture. And so do we.

Paul is not saying, "You used to conform to the pattern of this world." He is saying, "You already conform to the pattern of this world, and you don't even know it. Stop it!" The proof is in the words "any longer." Remember, Paul is writing to "brothers"—Christian men in Rome and to us!

Conform means agree with; match; be consistent with; measure up to; obey the rules; play the game; or take on the shape, behavior, or attitude of something.

The question is not, "Will you conform?" The question is, "To whom or what do you presently conform?"

No matter how tough or strong we think we are, we are still molded by the influences, powers, and principalities surrounding us. Everything strives to mold us into its image. That's why we are concerned with the quality of our children's friends: we know our kids are influenced by the company they keep. The number one reason people give for smoking is because their friends smoked. I'm sure the reason for other behaviors is the same.

Let's take the definition of *conform* and put it in our scripture phase: "Do not agree with; match; be consistent with; measure up to; obey the rules of; play the game of; or take on the shape, behavior, or attitude of the world—any longer." Ouch!

How does this rendition challenge you? How is it helpful to shed more light on this step in our growth? We must face our vulnerability to being molded. The thought of being molded by the pattern of this world is tough to accept and tougher to confess. That's why it is extremely necessary to do both—with God.

When Nehemiah rebuilt Jerusalem, he faced overwhelming opposition from enemies wanting Israel completely erased from the face of the earth. Nehemiah was outmanned and outgunned. The walls of Jerusalem had huge gaps, offering zero protection. Nehemiah went to work and identified the weak places in the walls; posted guards at each, and then rebuilt them.

> I stationed some of the people behind the lowest points of the wall at the exposed places. (Nehemiah 4:13; read verses 11–20 to know the context)

The Point: Identify the weak places in your walls. Guard them with prayer and ask God to rebuild your defenses.

- How are our lives like the unsaved men around us?
- How are our lives different from the unsaved men around us?
- How do the similarities hinder our witness?
- What must you become to end your conformity to the world?
- With whom can you discuss this devotional thought?

8

"Do not conform any longer to the pattern of this world …" (Romans 12:2)

I know a man who will not take his children to church because he does not want the church to brainwash them. He wants his kids to make their own decisions when they are older. Little does he realize he is brainwashing them to be just like himself. He is the mold; they are the clay.

God knows we are being molded every day. His concern is who or what is molding us. God's molding is for our best interest and holy.

What word identifies to what we must not conform?

A pattern is to be duplicated, copied, or followed. The Ford Motor Company built twelve new Model Ts a few years ago to celebrate their one hundredth anniversary. They combed through their archived drawings to find the originals so all the components they made would be original and not aftermarket parts. Then they gathered some original Model Ts and their owners to study how all the parts fit together. Ford disassembled a few of these Model Ts to make new drawings of the original components and to study the fit. They wanted the new versions to be *exactly* like the originals. The old Model T is the pattern to be duplicated, copied, and followed. The word *pattern* is generic, however the words used to describe the pattern have deadly importance.

"Of this world" is the dark description of the pattern to which we must not conform. *World* does not mean earth and created animals, minerals, or vegetables. *World* means "the realm of the unredeemed."

We must not conform to the pattern molding those who do not have a personal relationship with Jesus Christ.

The question now becomes, "To whom or what are we to conform?"

God establishes the pattern in Genesis 1:26. "Then God said, 'Let us make man in our image, in our likeness.'" There it is! "Created in God's image and likeness" boggles my mind! We must not conform to the realm of the unredeemed, and God wants us to conform to His image and likeness. The next question is how. That answer begins in tomorrow's devotional. But for now, let us ponder today's challenge.

The Point: Strive to understand the difference in being created in God's image and conforming to the pattern of the world. By doing so, we take a giant step toward understanding God's will for our lives.

- Read 2 Corinthians 5:17.
- Write this verse in your own words.
- What patterns in your life are similar to patterns in non-Christian men?
- What does being created in God's image look like to you?
- What patterns in your life copy God's image?
- How can we change this pattern to reflect God's likeness?
- With whom can you discuss this important truth?

9

"Do not conform any longer to the pattern of the world, but ..." (Romans 12:2)

We've heard this shoe drop before! The boss gives us a compliment and then says "but" before he or she dumps the real issue on us. The largest and heaviest *but* in the world stands between a compliment and a criticism. We understand *but* so well that anytime we receive a compliment, we shiver and respond by saying, "But what?" However, Paul did not set us up so he could drop a big *but* on us.

But opens the door to an alternative course of action or behavior. *Instead of* or *however* would better communicate the meaning of *but*, however God did not inspire me to write this letter.

> *But*—an opportunity to know, understand, and choose a transformed lifestyle.
>
> *But*—an explosion of grace because God offers what we do not deserve.
>
> *But*—an pouring out of mercy because God withholds the punishment we deserve.
>
> *But*—an offering of hope to a hopeless world.

Paul knew Christian men need to hear, examine, discuss, and implement the truth that follows. Paul believed men want to grow in their relationship with Christ and not just talk about it. Alpha Men want to know how to walk the talk and are willing to adjust their course to do so.

Elijah witnessed the unashamed rebellion against growing closer to God:

> Elijah went before the people and said, "How long will you waver between two opinions? If the Lord is God, follow him; but if Baal is god, follow him. But the people said nothing." (1 Kings 18:21)

But the people said nothing! Elijah challenged them with a call to repentance and growth, and they choose to remain rebelliously silent against God! Can you see their evil smirk?

The Point: Say something! Respond to God's call for transformation!

- Have you accepted Christ as your savior?
- If not, what is stopping you from doing so right now?
- What is the first step you must take to accepting Christ as your savior? It's the hardest and easiest thing you will ever do!
- How will implementing this truth change your daily life?
- List a way this truth enables you to grow your relationship with Christ.
- What will you do right now to begin your "walk the talk" experience?
- Whom can you share this amazing experience with right now?

10

"Do not conform any longer to the pattern of the world, but be transformed ..." (Romans 12:2)

The word *transform* in Greek means metamorphosis. The most common illustration is a caterpillar transforming into a butterfly. The late, great world heavyweight boxing champion Muhammad Ali said he "floats like a butterfly and stings like a bee." I like the manly "sting like a bee" part!

Transformation is a brick wall that men hit as they follow Christ toward alpha manhood. We misunderstand the concept, and so we resist it with all our masculinity because we think it will emasculate us. We resist because we buy into the pattern of this world's outward trail to manhood.

Transformation does not lessen your manliness or attack your masculine soul! You do not become weak, touchy-feely, or weepy-eyed. You won't speak with a higher pitched voice. Transformation will not change who you are. We still like football, fast cars, motorcycles, hunting, fishing, snowmobiles, ATVs, camping, backpacking, and one-inch-thick steaks off the grill. The difference is we reprioritize our lives and let all we do honor our heavenly Father. Transformation affects our priorities, which alters our behavior and motives (reasons driving your behavior).

Transformation enables us to see habits, entertainment, relationships, and behaviors from a new perspective—God's perspective. He gives us victory over all that plagues our lives! Will we always win? No. Will He always forgive us when we fail? Yes!

Does He want to free us from being a slave to our non-transformed behaviors? Yes! Does He want our lives to honor Him? Yes!

Transformation moves us from what we are to what God enables us to be.

> Men loved darkness instead of light because their deeds were evil …But whoever lives by the truth comes into the light, so that it may be seen plainly that what he has done has been done through God. (John 3:19, 21; read verses 16–21 for context; know the flow!)

Don't be discouraged. Many see changes in our lives before we do. Jesus taught,

> Ask and it will be given to you; seek and you will find; knock and the door will be open to you. For everyone who asks receives; he who seeks finds; and to him who knocks, the door will be open. (Matthew 7:7–8)

The Point: Embrace transformation. Do not hesitate. It is God's way of making you the best Alpha Man you can be!

- What motivates you to seek God's transformation? Why?
- What hinders you from seeking God's transformation? Why?
- What must you put under Christ's authority so that you may be transformed?
- How will you explain your transformation to your coworker, spouse, or child?

11

> "Do not conform any longer to the pattern of the world, but be transformed by the renewing of your mind ..." (Romans 12:2)

I like the TV game show *Jeopardy*, where the contestants formulate questions based on the answers. I am still amazed at the vast amount of information contestants know.

The answer is, "By the renewing of your mind." What's the question?

You are correct! "How can I not conform to the pattern of the world any longer?"

The answer, renewing, raises the question, "How?" The Bible answers this question too! As we regularly read and think about God's Word, it reprograms (renews) our minds. We begin to understand God's perspective, see through God's eyes, hear through God's ears, and think with the mind of Christ. In other words, we begin to experience what it means to be transformed into the image and likeness of God.

> Finally, brothers, whatever is true, whatever is noble, whatever is right, whatever is pure, whatever is lovely, whatever is admirable—if anything is excellent or praiseworthy—*think about such things.* (Philippians 4:8; emphasis added)

Here are a few more scriptures for renewing your mind.

Do not let this Book of the Law depart from your mouth: meditate on it day and night." (Joshua 1:8)

Your attitude should be the same as that of Christ Jesus. (Philippians 2:5)

You were taught …to be made new in the attitude of your minds. (Ephesians 4:22–23)

There's the key! Thinking reprograms (renews) our minds. When we think about God's Word, God's ways, and God's holiness, we more clearly understand our need of transformation into His likeness. As we think about God's attributes, the Holy Spirit transforms our thinking, which transforms our behaviors and lives. That, my friend, is a renewal we all need!

The Point: Think about such things!

- Why is it important to understand God's perspective?
- Why is it important to understand God's attributes?
- What do you usually think about throughout the day?
- Name a behavior or attitude each "whatever" in Philippians 4:8 embraces.
- Pick one "whatever" to think about today. Be intentional!
- Which "whatever" will you share with a brother to help him grow?

12

"Do not conform any longer to the pattern of the world, but be transformed by the renewing of your mind. Then you will be able to test and approve what God's will is—His good, pleasing and perfect will." (Romans 12:2)

"The proof is in the pudding" can be interpreted as, "Did the formula work?" Did we get the desired results? Is the reward worth the effort and expense to create it?

With a renewed mind, we have a mindset enabling us to test God's leadership. By saying *test*, Paul does not mean we will determine whether God passes or fails. He means we apply God's principles to our lives to discover the benefits and blessings He offers. By testing God's principles, we know the final product is worth the effort (discipline) it took to implement it. We are being tested, not God. We are proving God's ways works and our ways do not.

Before our renewed minds, we are like the Israelites in Jeremiah's time. Jeremiah told them the Lord was angry because of their sins, and he promised harsh judgment unless they repented. The Israelites answered:

> "We will not listen to the message you have spoken to us in the Name of the Lord. We will certainly do everything we said we would." (Jeremiah 44:16–17; read the entire chapter to know the ugly flow)

These Israelites were determined to do what God forbade them to do because they refused to renew their minds. They committed to stay conformed to the pattern of the world and refused to be transformed. They refused to know His good, pleasing, and perfect will for their lives. They refused to repent.

However in Joshua's day, Israel had a different mindset, revealed in their response to Joshua's message from the Lord.

> Whatever you have commanded us we will do, and wherever you send us we will go. Just as we fully obeyed Moses, so we will obey you. (Joshua 1:16)

The only way we experience His good, pleasing and perfect will is to allow the Holy Spirit to renew our minds and permit God to work His will in us. As we invest time reading and studying His Word and hearing the Word preached, we position ourselves to receive His blessing of knowledge and depth of insight (wisdom).

The Point: Obeying God's leadership is the only way to prove His good, pleasing and perfect will for our lives. Offer God the Joshua 1:16 response to His call. Do it now!

- Write down five benefits to knowing His good, pleasing and perfect will.
- How will each of these benefits improve your walk with God?
- What must you do to test or prove God's will for your life is the best choice?
- Who can help you understand this principle?

Memory System: On a 3×5 index card, write a Bible verse, including the book, chapter, and verse. Keep it in your pocket and several times during the day read it. Within one week you will have the verse and reference memorized. Start with Romans 12:1–2!

Second Principle

Do not think of yourself more highly than you ought. (Romans 12:3b)

COMMENTARY

For by the grace given me I say to every one of you: Do not think of yourself more highly than you ought, but rather think of yourself with sober judgment, in accordance with the faith God has given you. Just as each of us has one body with many members, and these members do not all have the same function, so in Christ we, who are many, form one body, and each member belongs to all the others. We have different gifts, according to the grace given us. If a man's gift is prophesying, let him use it in proportion to his faith; ⁷if it is serving, let him serve; if it is teaching, let him teach; if it is encouraging, let him encourage; if it is distributing to the needs of others, let him give generously; if it is leadership, let him govern diligently; if it is showing mercy, let him do it cheerfully. (Romans 12:3a, 3c–8)

13

"For by the grace given me I say to every one of you …" (Romans 12:3a)

The old Mac Davis song says, "Oh, Lord it's hard to be humble when you're perfect in every way." It's funny because it is supposed to be. Some of our dads sang this to annoy us. If you do not know this song, do *not* google it. Your kids will appreciate you *not* singing it.

Paul's humility powerfully levels the playing field. After reading Paul's brief résumé in Philippians 3:4–7, you'll understand his credentials could fuel arrogance. When you add his church planting record, hundreds of souls coming to know Christ through his ministry, and his Roman citizenship, it's amazing he remained humble at all. However, Paul's mind was transformed and renewed. The Holy Spirit reigned in his heart and ruled his life. He learned to think like God thinks, see like God sees, and love like God loves. He viewed his life from God's perspective and knew the man he was today was the result of God's ongoing transforming power pulsating through his life.

Paul knew he could deliver this message because God transformed him and gave him the ability to do so. "It's not about me, it's all about Thee!" When we truly believe this, we move toward humility.

About Jesus, John the Baptist said, "He must become greater; I must become less" (John 3:30). This is humility defined in the best street theology you will ever find!

Humility shouts we are no better than those to whom we speak. Our story is about God working in and through us, and it's not because we are special, unique, or a cut above everyone else. If God stops working in our lives, we fall faster than a lead balloon. Our story must say to others, "What God is doing in me, He can also do in you!"

Paul believed Christians men actively seek a renewed mind and hunger to know more about a closer brotherhood with Christ. He was also climbing off the pedestal the Roman Christians had put him on because they thought his church-planting success was all about Paul. He wanted them to know God was using him to spread the gospel among the Gentiles.

The Point: When we share what God is doing in our lives, we share God's story—not ours. It's not about us; it never has been, is not right now, and never will be. It's always about God! Thank God for the accomplishments He is doing in your life. Let your humility praise God right now. True humility always precedes holy praise!

- What makes you more special in God's eyes than non-Christian men?
- Why do you think God loves you more than these?
- When you give God total, absolute credit for His work in your life, how will your story change?
- How are you giving God permission to renew your mind and transform your life?
- Can you explain the difference between confidence and arrogance?
- Discuss why you are ready to continue your Alpha Manhood journey.

14

"Do not think of yourself more highly than you ought …" (Romans 12:3b)

I attended an assembly where the speaker illustrated this concept. He told us to clap our hands one time on the count of three. He then counted, "One … two," and clapped his hands. All of us did the same. Then he said, "Three," and clapped his hands again. We got the point! People do what they see and not what they're told.

Paul's first phase defined his life. I'm confident they heard about his successful church-planting ministry and the hundreds of souls won to Christ. Paul knew human nature favors hero worship. However, Paul knew he was just a man, born in sin and redeemed by the blood of Christ shed on Calvary. He was no better or worse than those to whom he was writing.

Today's verse is the border guard between the states of confidence and arrogance.

First, notice Paul did not say, "Do not think of yourself." If he said this, how would you interpret this verse?

Second, "more highly than you ought" explains and qualifies the first five words in the context. What questions pop into your mind? What words need clarifying? What concepts need exploring? Here are some thoughts to consider.

1) "More highly" tells me it is okay to have confidence and faith, but not arrogance of the flesh; read Philippians 3:1–11.

2) Thinking "more highly than we ought," suggests we cross from confidence into arrogance because we take credit for all we have done, as if Christ made a less important contribution than our own.

How does Philippians 4:13 clarify today's verse?

"I can do everything through him who gives me strength."

3) Is Paul confident or arrogant? Based on Philippians 4:13, what does "do everything" mean to you?
4) How about David's many statements when he saw Israel's army quivering in fear because of Goliath's challenge in 1 Samuel 17?
5) Is David confident and full of faith, or is he arrogant and cocky? Why or why not?
6) Is he speaking faith or bragging about his human abilities to make this happen?

Explain the difference.

7) "Than you ought" makes me ask, What does *ought* mean? It does not mean something is optional. It means a duty or obligation. But duty or obligation to what or whom? Why or why not be obligated?

The Point: Thinking is hard work. Thinking properly is harder and less comfortable. Don't opt out. Think!

✐ Answer each question scattered throughout this devotional.
✐ Remember to process this in the light provided by Romans 12:1–2.

15

"But rather think of yourself with sober judgment ..."
(Romans 12:3c)

I have seen more than my share of alcoholism at its worse: stammering, slobbering, staggering men and women losing all control of their bodies and mouths. It is an ugly, sickening, fearful sight! The slick TV and print ads do not reveal the horrible dark side of this destructive, socially acceptable, addictive, substance-abusing behavior. I wish I could erase these films from my cranial DVD library.

Sober means in control; not polluted by negative influences; based on principles proven to be true over time and across cultural, racial, economic and political barriers.

Judgment is the ability to make factual decisions. Judgment is a double-edged sword. One edge brings blessings and quality of life to the one making decisions based on God's Word and will. The other edge brings wrath and destruction to the one making decisions rejecting God's authority in one's life.

Anything standing between you and your obedience to God's revealed will is a god in your life, and we know how God feels that. God refuses to play second fiddle! The foundation of humanism is, "I am in control of my life. No one tells me what to do. I determine the direction of my life. I make me successful. I answer to no one. I decide what is right for me." "I ...me ...my"—these are the supreme pronouns used to declare this humanistic view of self-rule.

Sober judgment is impossible when we serve self under the guise that we are serving God.

So what happens if an "I…me…my" man marries an "I…me…my" wife? And what if they have two "I…me…my" kids? Then "I…me…my" becomes "My oh my, what a war!"

Once again, the big *but* lives on! In this case, I interpret *but* to mean instead. Does this make sense to you?

> Do not think more highly of yourself than you ought, *instead* think of yourself with sober judgment.

It's time to choose again! How do we think about ourselves? Do we use sober judgment based on God's principles? Or are we drunk on the "I…me…my" elixir and excuse our self-serving judgment by saying, "After all, God made me this way." As if that lead balloon flies!

The Point: We must Alpha Man up and examine how we think about ourselves, in view of God's mercy and with sober judgment using our renewed minds.

- ✎ What is the measuring rod, or standard, you use to judge yourself?
- ✎ Before you answer, check out Isaiah's response to his vision of God in Isaiah 6:1–13. Pay close attention to verse 6.
- ✎ Why do we tend to be more understanding and forgiving for our own faults than we do the faults of others?
- ✎ What do you think your accountability partner will say about this?

16

"In accordance with the measure of faith God has given you." (Romans 12:3d)

As the assistant pastor, I stood before the congregation to receive the offering. Wanting to issue a brief challenge concerning tithing, I prayerfully walked to the pulpit and said,

> I believe many 1 percent, 3 percent and 5 percent Christians are sprinkled among us this morning. Christians who do not believe they can afford to tithe a full 10 percent. I believe every Christian wants to tithe.
>
> Romans 12:3 says to think about ourselves "in accordance with the measure of faith God has given to you." So I issue this challenge.
>
> This morning, give your tithe in accordance with your measure of 1, 3, or 5 percent faith. Do this for two weeks, and then add 1 percent to your faith tithe the following week. In two weeks, add another 1 percent as you continue your climb to reach 10 percent. It's easier than you think!
>
> Begin where you are and intentionally grow to where God wants you to be!

After the worship service, three people came to me and told me they tithed at the percentage they believe expressed their level of faith, and they promised to follow the growth plan. Within four weeks, they told me they were tithing a full 10 percent!

Concerning tithing, the measure of faith is 10 percent of your income. Please note tithing is only one of many spiritual disciplines we must develop. Prayer, Bible reading, serving others, and discovering and using your spiritual gifts are other spiritual disciplines we tackle as we move closer to our Lord.

What is the measuring rod you use to judge your level of faith? Based on a scale of 1–10 estimate your measure of faith: ___ percent.

Do not be hard on yourself—your faith is greater than you think! After all, it is not about you or your abilities. It is about God empowering and leading you to higher ground. This discussion is to stir your faith so you continually trust Christ and strive for steady growth in Him.

The Point: With a renewed mind, you see more clearly how to fulfill your place in God's plan. For some disciplines, the standard is daily. For others, it is continually.

- What area in your life needs intentional, progressive, spiritual growth?
- If daily means every day and continually means moment by moment, which one is best for your faith walk? Why or why not?
- What do you have to do to establish a daily or continual disciplined walk?
- When will you start?
- Whom can you enlist to walk this walk with you?

17

"Just as each of us has one body with many members, and these members do not all have the same function …" (Romans 12:4)

To better understand the interconnectivity of your various bodily components, hit your finger with a hammer. This action immediately brings your entire body to a screeching halt while everything within focuses on one little, solitary member. Your body refuses to function as designed. Your brain has only one single thought as time freezes, and nothing else exists within your paradigm except your finger.

The reality of your body being comprised of thousands of members, each with its own individualized function, is not hard to grasp and has become a boring piece of body trivia. This is also true in our churches and men's ministries.

To generate excitement, all members must work together to reach a common goal or complete a common task. When the entire body functions as a team, great things are accomplished!

With hands gripping a hickory stick, arms cocked and loaded for rapid deployment, feet shoulder's width apart, body weight on the back foot, eyes focused on the rawhide-wrapped sphere of string, breathing controlled, and ears shutting out all extemporaneous noises, the entire unified body waits for the exact moment in time when the power in every individual member is released in perfect unity so the hickory stick makes solid contact with the sphere of string to accomplish its singular, unified goal. When everything is working together in intentional, disciplined harmony, the result is the announcer screaming into the microphone, "It's gone! It's outta here! Home run! Tigers win! Tigers win!"

> We can do great things as individuals and greater things as a team!

This verse addresses the strength and talent Joe brings to the team—and what is lost if he leaves. Look at any sports team. When a player goes down, someone will succeed him yet may not be able to replace him. There's a huge difference!

With a renewed mind, we see people through God's eyes, meaning we value the person above what he brings to the team. Yes, we value and appreciate his strengths and talents, however above everything else, we value him as a person, as a brother in Christ.

The Points: 1) Every man brings something to the team, even if only himself.
2) Value the man above his skill set.

- Explain the difference between succeeding and replacing a team member.
- Have you left the team?
- What will you do to rejoin the team?
- Name a man who is absent from your team.
- What will you do to get him back?
- When will you reach out to him to encourage him to return?
- Who can help you?

18

"So in Christ we who are many form one body …"
(Romans 12:5)

"What happens in Vegas stays in Vegas" is a sad commentary on our society. The idea that what happens in one area of our lives does not effect the other areas is an invitation to violate your integrity, commitments, vows, and character in faux security and secrecy without any consequences. It's situation ethics reaching its most destructive apex. Even though no one else knows, you and God always know, bringing guilt, condemnation, and ugly consequences.

This is the polar opposite of what today's verse teaches. The word *so* means because verse four is true, what follows is the logical result. "In Christ" describes how we form one body. Each NFL team has many members, yet they function as one so when the tackle maintains the block and the quarterback connects with the wide receiver, the entire team scores. The same is true with our men's group and church. We who are in Christ are one team. Pat Riley, former Los Angeles Lakers head coach, said it well: "When the ball goes through the hoop it takes ten hands to put it there." When the team wins, everyone gets a hash mark in the win column!

With this attitude, the entire team becomes a force ready to overcome any challenge and defeat any foe, as Acts 2:1 perfectly illustrates: "When the day of Pentecost came, they were all together in one place."

"All together in one place" looks redundant until you understand the difference. "In one place" means in the same geographical location—the upper room in Jerusalem. Each chose to "stay in the city until you have been clothed with power from on high" (Luke 23:49b).

"All together" means they have one heart. They collectively commit to receive "what my Father has promised" (Luke 49a). They believe Christ and are determined to receive the promise of being "clothed with power from on high." One body, one heart, one goal.

Approximately 500 people saw the resurrected Christ, yet only about 120 chose to stay in the city until they received the power from on high Jesus promised—and those who stayed changed history! The legacy of this humble, power-filled handful of men and women is recorded in the rest of the New Testament. It is still being fulfilled today by those who "stay in the city until you have been clothed with power from on high."

The Point: What happens in Jerusalem must *not* stay in Jerusalem!

> Therefore go and make disciples of all nations, baptizing them in the name of the Father and of the Son and of the Holy Spirit. and teaching them to obey everything I have commanded you. And surely I am with you always, to the very end of the age. (Matthew 28:19)

- What will you do so you can be clothed with power from on high?
- Are you one with others in your quest to experience this infilling power?
- What will it take for your group to be all together in one place?
- How will you lead your group to be all together in one place?

19

"And each member belongs to all the others." (Romans 12:5)

Way back in the 1960s, I was a paperboy and had to collect each week from my customers. Some coins from the late 1800s and early 1900s were still in circulation, and this motivated me to start a coin collection. Morgan dollars, Mercury dimes, Buffalo nickels, copper and steel Lincoln Wheat cents, Standing Liberty quarters, and half dollars were regularly used for payment. Those were the days!

As the design, material, and weight of the coins changed, I did not mix the new coins with the older ones because I felt the new coins did not belong. Being coins was what they had in common.

I did not consciously segregate these coins in my mind; it happened naturally and with no effort at all. I justified keeping the old and new coins in different containers by thinking the new coins were not as good as the older ones. If we are not careful, we will think about other men this way.

Men are like coins and are different by race, nationality, education, income, generation, clothing style, language, vocation, culture, face and body type, and hair style. Even though we are human and of masculine gender, men are different. This verse addresses the belonging of each man to one another, not the differences.

Webster's Dictionary defines *belong* as to be attached or bound by birth, allegiance, or dependency.

Men judge by the outside, but God looks upon the heart. The definition for *belongs* is crucial for our understanding of this verse. All

Christian men, from all walks of life, belong to one another. Here's the phrase with the definition injected into it.

> And each member is attached or bound by birth, allegiance or dependency to all the others.

Attached or bound by birth (in Christ), allegiance (to Christ), or dependency (on Christ) to each other. Without Christ, we are all just a bunch of coins in a bag. However, with Christ we become a fortress bound together by the mortar of His Holy Spirit and our renewed minds. All men belong. If "all" does not mean "all", then what does "all" mean?

Paul cuts through the junk separating us from those who are different. The transformed mind realizes that whether friend or foe, all men belong to each other.

The Point: It is up to us to show other men they belong in our group no matter how different we seem to be. It's our responsibility, not theirs.

- How does The Point change your understanding of this verse?
- What do you do to help every man know he belongs in your group?
- How do you communicate acceptance to those who are different?
- Is your acceptance genuine to the core or simply political correctness?
- What can God do to improve your level of total acceptance?

20

"We have different gifts according to the grace given us …" (Romans 12:6)

While in high school, my brother worked at a men's clothing store. His employers very quickly learned Ray had a gift for knowing what clothes sold well and how to match them for a very cool, contemporary, mid-sixties look. Whether dressing for the board room or the street scene, Ray had the gift. It wasn't long before the owners relied on Ray to order all the inventory, and they watched their profits rise. As the non-cool little brother of this very hip haberdasher, I depended on his gift, but I soon learned stylish clothing could only take me so far.

This verse reaches back to verse four, "and these members do not all have the same function." By expanding this concept, we understand our gifts come from God and not from genetics: "according to the grace *given* us." By God's grace (giving us what we do not deserve), we are instilled with an embryo of talent needing to grow to bring glory to the Giver and blessings those who receive the benefits of our gifts.

Many churches fail at this point. We look at the man, and based on *our* needs, we put him in a place where he can be useful to *our* agenda. However, when we help him discover his gifts, he excels in his ministry. We are in such a hurry to plug a hole in *our* ministry plan that we fail to fill the position with men gifted for that task. Growing churches take time and commit resources enabling men to discover their spiritual gifts so they can minister from their strengths and not struggle in their weaknesses.

When Alpha Males use their spiritual gifts, the Church experiences power and adventure needed to impact their communities. Adventure is missing in many churches today. Men's souls are energized by the Word of God when it is preached, taught, and applied from a masculine point of view. Jesus is not a female in a male body! He's the greatest Alpha Man to walk on the face of earth. When church leaders realize this and proclaim "the Man, Christ Jesus," more men will join His team.

The bottom line is that when Alpha Males struggle to serve, we quit serving. Our fear of failure is too overwhelming for us to continue. We do not look for the easy but the impossible made possible by faith. We believe we can conquer any challenge with God's help and in a masculine way. Men want a challenged without being told how to do it. Men look for adventure because we're wired for it. We invite men to our twenty-mile backpacking trip before we invite them to Sunday school or men's group. Backpacking is masculine, whereas Sunday school and men's group is perceived as being for the weak.

How do we help men discover their spiritual gifts? Most studies are designed for classroom settings, and men learn best by thinking on their feet and performing hands-on activities. A curriculum writer's greatest challenge is how to change the method without compromising the message. The only thing at stake is the masculine soul and future growth of the Church.

The Point: Men do not want a feminine Jesus! Present Jesus as the ultimate Alpha Male!

- What are your spiritual gifts?
- How do you use them in ministry?
- How does your church teach men to discover their spiritual gifts?
- How does your church allow men to use their spiritual gifts in manly ways?
- What can you do to help men discover their spiritual gifts?

21

"We have different gifts, according to the grace given us. If a man's gift is prophesying, let him use it in proportion to his faith. If serving, let him serve; if it is teaching, let him teach; if it is encouraging, let him encourage; if it is contributing to the needs of others, let him give generously; if it is leadership, let him govern diligently; if it is showing mercy let him do it cheerfully." (Romans 12:6–8)

"Just do it!" The famous trademark of Nike cuts through all our excuses and whining. It moves us from spectating to participating in sports, exercise, and life. "Just do it!" encourages us to quit stalling and get it done. In doing, we learn the skills needed to be successful. In other words, Alpha Man-UP!

Tom Landry, former head coach of the Dallas Cowboys, said it was his job to make players do what they did not want to do, when they do not want to do it, in a way they did not want to do it, and to do it consistently. Each player can improve his performance when he intentionally practices to elevate his game. Every player must believe he can improve and practice to that end!

A player blessed with enough talent to be the best can easily fall into the disastrous pit of complacency. Complacency assumes you don't need to change, seeks stress-free comfort, and is deaf and blind to the enemy's determination to steal your talent and destroy you in the process. Complacency is driving with your eyes closed.

Paul's list is not exhaustive but is representative. His focus was not on the nouns or the verbs (prophesying, serve, teach, etc.). His focus was on the verb *let*, "to give permission and opportunity" (Free Online Dictionary).

We are many members with different gifts, and so it's logical to think each member uses his gifts to the benefit of the entire body. However, this is not always true. Many churches and pastors want men to plug into the established plan. The "do it my way" ministry is one person thinking he has all the answers, and he alone knows the best way to minister to others.

Read verses 6–8 again and use the definition instead of the word *let*.

> serving, give him permission and opportunity to serve.

We are living sacrifices, no longer conforming to the pattern of the world, being transformed by the renewing of our mind, thinking about ourselves with sober judgment in accordance with our measure of faith, having different gifts given by God's grace, and belonging to one another. We must "give permission and opportunity" to each alpha male to use his gifts in order to build God's kingdom!

The Point: All men need to serve is permission and opportunities to use their gifts. Create opportunities and grant permission for Alpha Males to use their gifts and skills.

- How does giving permission look?
- How does creating opportunity look to men?
- How does this new understanding change how you minister to and with men?
- How does this change your personal ministry?

Your spiritual gifts empower you for maximum service in God's Kingdom Building activities!

If we don't know what tools are in our toolbox, how can we use them?

I went through a few spiritual gift Bible studies at our church, and I must admit I did not discover my spiritual gifts while sitting in a classroom discussing the material. We men learn best from hands-on experiences. How did you learn to fix your car? By helping your dad, doing it yourself, or reading a book? My friend disassembled the automatic transmission in his Chevy Blazer and put each piece in a paper bag numbered in the order he removed the parts. To reassemble the transmission, he simply installed the parts in the opposite order. The transmission worked, and he drove his Blazer for another five years. He never owned, read, or glanced at a transmission repair manual.

The Point: Men learn best by doing, so involve our hand and teach us to serve.

Many people only talk about their faith. This creates weak, ineffective, talking-head Christians who talk a good game but can't deliver the goods.

Business has the 80/20 principle: 20 percent of the workers generate 80 percent of the sales. I decided to test this theory.

I tracked the 80/20 principle in churches where I served as pastor or on staff. I discovered 20 percent of our attendance gave 80 percent of our finances, made up 80 percent of our volunteers, and invited 80 percent of our visitors to church.

Next, I expanded my research by reviewing two-years stats of the 77 churches on our district, using monthly morning attendance, Sunday school enrollment and Sunday school attendance figures, and money raised by each church. I discovered 20 percent (fifteen) of our churches generated 80 percent of the totals in each of these areas! So how does this apply to our men's group?

The Point: When we motive an additional 10 percent of our men to get involved in ministry, we multiply our outreach effectiveness and velocity of growth. In other words, we grow like the church in the book of Acts, adding daily those being saved.

Moving men from the 80 percent into the top 20 percent is our challenge as we lead men to become biblical Alpha Males. We must be willing to act in spite of our fears. We must move, live, and operate outside our personal comfort zones. We must become willing to do what we have never done before in order to become what we have never been: Biblical Alpha Males.

This is not about human strength. It's about faith in God to strengthen us as we sightlessly walk into the unknown by faith. Alpha Males must muster up the courage, intensify their determination, and force themselves to do what must be done in order to achieve what they crave to gain. Courage is action in spite of fear. Biblical courage is only possible with a life transformed, a mind renewed, and God's Holy Spirit empowering us from within.

Don't quit here, brother! Man up and keep walking!

This naturally leads us to examine two more questions: How and How.

How[1]? Ask clarifying questions.

- What ministry looks fun? (For me, this is number one)
- What ministry looks easy? (A close number two)
- About what ministry am I curious?
- How can I make my hobby into a ministry?
- What ministry event do I enjoy attending?
- What ministry stirs up my mind with ideas to improve it?
- With what ministry leader(s) do I share these ideas?
- What ministry do I think I could do well?
- About what ministry have I thought or said, "If I were in charge, I would …"?
- What ministry do I support financially in addition to my tithes?
- If I had to choose a ministry to do, what would I choose?

If my curiosity challenges me to learn about a ministry, many times this is God's leading me toward that ministry. What other questions help you clarify your thoughts?

The Point: By asking clarifying questions, the Lord guides your thoughts to the ministries He gifted you to perform.

How[2]? Volunteer to help in a ministry that How[1] revealed as a possible match for you.

- Ask God to guide you. This basic first step in all eternal adventures.
- Ask God to help the current leaders and volunteers in this ministry.

- Ask God to bless the people to whom this ministry is given.
- Sit in and watch the leader and volunteers perform the ministry.
- Read about the ministry you are willing to try. (I know you don't like to read. Just get over it!)
- Commit to a six-week trial. I discovered this is ample time to give my best shot. Buck fever is not just for deer hunters.
- Ask how and why questions to those involved in this ministry.
- Speak with people experienced in the ministry to stir up your curiosity.
- Think about this ministry throughout the day.
- Always, always look for ways to improve your skill level.
- Tell yourself "Just Do It!" until you do!
- Read another book! Never stop learning!

I'm not gifted in some ministries, such as preschool ministries. However, I taught junior boys and senior adults. I led ten mission teams to four countries; sang in choirs, small groups, and solos; developed outreach and follow-up ministries; served as senior, assistant, and youth pastor; and worked as a worship leader and senior adult director.

I also served on district and general church leadership councils. I faced each new adventure with feelings of inadequacies, some degree of fear of failing, and a gut-wrenching determination to do what I had to do in order to succeed.

The Point: It's amazing what God does through an Alpha Male willing to try what he believes he cannot do at an inconvenient time. It's astonishing what we can do when it's just God and me!

- What are you willing to do to join the productive, top 20 percent?
- Respond to of the How[1] questions listed above.
- Respond to each of the How[2] questions listed above.
- What will you do to discuss your understanding with a friend?

- What are you willing to do to discuss this with your men's group?
- After discovering our spiritual gifts, what is the first step you must take to use your gifts to benefit the entire body?
- What are the second and third steps?

The Point: Men desperately need camaraderie and encouragement from other men. Many churches do ministry focusing on women but not men. You need Christian brothers, and they need you. Yes, I'm trying to start an open-minded discussion.

Third Principle

Love must be sincere. (Romans 12:9a)

COMMENTARY

Hate what is evil; cling to what is good. Be devoted to one another in love. Honor one another above yourselves. Never be lacking in zeal, but keep your spiritual fervor, serving the Lord. Be joyful in hope, patient in affliction, faithful in prayer. Share with the Lord's people who are in need. Practice hospitality. Bless those who persecute you; bless and do not curse. Rejoice with those who rejoice; mourn with those who mourn. Live in harmony with one another. Do not be proud, but be willing to associate with people of low position. Do not be conceited. Do not repay anyone evil for evil. Be careful to do what is right in the eyes of everyone. If it is possible, as far as it depends on you, live at peace with everyone. Do not take revenge, my friends, but leave room for God's wrath, for it is written: "It is mine to avenge; I will repay," says the Lord. On the contrary: "If your enemy is hungry, feed him; if he is thirsty, give him something to drink. In doing this, you will heap burning coals on his head. Do not be overcome by evil, but overcome evil with good. (Romans 12:9b–21)

22

"Love …" Romans 12:9

I love my wife, kids, church, and my 2001 Ford Mustang GT. I love the United States, Barbados, Jamaica, and Brazil. I love clean air, the beach, and good food. But does love mean the same in each?

Here are definitions for the most significant Greek words used to translate *love*.

1. Agape: undefiled, unconditional, without hypocrisy; not influenced or affected by the person to whom it is directed. (used 147 times in the New Testament)

You cannot make God love you more or less than He does right now. Check out 1 Corinthians 13 for defining action verbs!

2. Phileos: brotherly; friendly affection, kindness expressed to one another; having things in common; a general type of love (used 42 times in the New Testament)

3. Eros: sexual love; from *eros* we get the word erotic (never used in Scripture).

4. Storge: Family Love (used only in Romans 12:10)

Care to guess which one of the *love* words is used in today's verse? We too quickly think of love as a noun when it is very clear when viewed as a verb. The noun *love* is conceptual, vague, fluid, and nondescript. However, as a verb it is an easily understood action. When you think of love, do you see a noun or a verb?

Men and women express love in gender-specific ways.

Examples: My wife wants me to tell her how I feel about her. I tell her by providing a house, car, clothing, and more.

She talks about keeping our family together. I help our daughters move out and be independent.

She dicusses problems. I solve them.

Our challenge is recognizing masculine expressions of love toward Christian brothers that respects and honors our masculine souls. Masculine expressions of love include a handshake, helping with a car or home repair, lawn work, giving a ride to work, an invitation to golf, fishing, ATV riding, and more.

The Point: Masculine expressions of love involve more action and less talk.

- How would masculine, unconditional, masculine love change your ministry to men?
- How can you express masculine love toward other men?
- Name a man who needs Christian brothers to care for him.
- What kind of masculine care does he need?
- How can we help men understand and practice this growth step?

23

"Love must ..." (Romans 12:9)

In high school, a kid retired from his morning paper route, and so I accepted his offer to take it over. It was perfect! I started a city block from home, and forty-five minutes later, I delivered the last paper across the street from my house.

My competitor and I began our deliveries at 7:00 a.m. To grow my route, I realized I must do something my competition wasn't doing. Our newspapers printed the same state and national news, had minor news coverage of our town, and cost the same. What could I do to gain a competitive edge?

I discovered the answer when I changed my question from "What can I do?" to "What must I do?"

My newspapers were at my pickup site at 4:15 a.m., and so I picked up my papers at 4:30, finishing my route by 5:30 a.m., one and a half hours before my competition began his route. Feedback from my customers was very positive and rewarding.

- They enjoyed receiving the newspaper before they left for work.
- Some took the newspaper with them to work.
- They told their neighbors about my early delivery, prompting a few to subscribe.
- I was back in bed one and a half hours before I had to get ready for school.

My success sparked Brainstorm 2.0. I requested enough free newspapers to deliver to every home on my route for two weeks. Once approved, we set a date for my delivery blitz. I paid a friend half of my weekly twelve-dollar commission to help. (In 1965, $6.00 was a lot of money!) After the blitz, I knocked on every door, telling them I delivered the *Charleston Gazette* to them free with no obligation, and I asked if they enjoyed the early delivery. Then I pulled the trigger and asked if they would like to continue receiving it for only $1.25 per week. I added eighteen new daily and twenty new Sunday-only subscribers. My income jumped 30 percent!

Changing *can* to *must* caused my juvenile thought process to shift gears, enabling me to trump my competition. "Love must" presents this same principle. *Can* addresses our ability and possibility; *must* addresses our duty, obligation, and course of action. *Can* is lazy and requires no action, only talk; *must* demands action with urgency.

Our churches are full of people who can do but have no urgency. *Can* address potential; *must* propels us into participation. Changing the question from "What can be done?" to "What must be done?" changes our lives, our churches, and our communities for Christ.

The Point: When you change the question, you change the answer, the direction, and the velocity.

- How does changing *can* to *must* challenge your ministry?
- What thoughts are stirred up within your mind right now?
- Specifically, what can be done in your ministry?
- Specifically, What must be done in your ministry?
- List the differences.
- What thoughts do you think Jesus has on this subject?

24

"Love must be sincere." (Romans 12:9)

Very early in life, I learned to use specific words, the right tone of voice, and facial expressions to convince others I was sincere even when I was not. It worked best when I had to apologize or needed to manipulate others for my benefit. I worked hard to learn how to play the game at the expert's level. After all, it was all about me.

I also discovered behaviors learned in one's youth stick well into adulthood and are very hard to discard. Only by God's grace could I break free and become sincere.

The word *sincere* means "without fillers." Clay pot makers filled the cracks after the pots were fired and before they were painted, making them look flawless. The crack filler was not as strong as the clay, and so when the pots were heated, the filler would fall out, making the pots useless. Where is the Consumer Protection Agency when you need it?

Isn't "undefiled, unconditional love without hypocrisy" the same as "sincere and without fillers?" My mind floats to the very obvious answer. So why the double-dip command?

A man not "transformed by the renewing of his mind" needs this double emphasis to shed light on the filler used in his cracked agape pot. James 1:8 says a man who lacks wisdom (seeing things from God's perspective) "is a double-minded man, unstable in all he does." He is not dependable or consistent, and so when heat is applied, he fails. You know what a man is made of when he is in the fire!

Once again, love is best understood as a verb, not a noun. Change the nouns in 1 Corinthians 13 to verbs to reveal how agape love looks when it is fleshed out in a man's daily walk with God. Try it!

Agape love is impossible to flesh out using human strength. We are cracked pots, and so we must ask God to make us the sincere alpha males He is calling us to become.

Today's verse says, "Love must be sincere." undefiled, unconditional, and without hypocrisy. Without fillers is a command, not an option. "Love must" is in present tense, so it must not be put off until a more convenient season.

The Point: The command is clear. Be sincere—no fillers!

- Define each verb in 1 Corinthians 13.
- How does changing the nouns in 1 Corinthians 13 to verbs affect your understanding of what love means?
- What in your expressions of love toward other men must change?
- How can you communicate this refreshed understanding to other Christian men?

Let's talk to God. "Father, my love is not sincere, and I can't make it sincere. I ask You to transform my life by renewing my mind with Your Word and Holy Spirit. I accept Your transformation. Make it so in me! In Jesus's name I pray. Amen."

25

"Love must be sincere. Hate what is evil …" (Romans 12:9)

"Never say *hate*, because it is a terrible word!" my mother said to me more times than I can count. I wonder if Mary said this to Jesus during his growing years.

Hate is a powerful, passionate emotion if we bathe it in God's righteousness and aim it toward finding solutions for the troubles men face. Hate is also a very powerful, positive emotion to harness for good.

Webster's Online Dictionary defines hate as:

> a: intense hostility and aversion usually deriving from fear, anger, or sense of injury
> b: extreme dislike or antipathy

When we understand hate as a verb, this says, "Hate (have intense hostility, aversion, extreme dislike for) what is evil."

God's character has no evil, and so His love is 100 percent holy—sinless and pure, without artificial colors, flavors, or fillers. Focus on the definition of hate and not the interpretations, and you will discover exciting truth.

> Because God is 100 percent holy, the prophet Habakkuk wrote, "Your eyes are too pure to look on evil; you cannot tolerate wrong." (Habakkuk 1:13)

What does this say to you concerning our personal, secret sins? How do we hate (take action against) sin? What does our hate of sin look like to men around us? What behaviors will grow out of our hate of sin? How can God express His hate of sin through us? Not modified behavior, but transformed hearts birthing behavior changes.

The first step to recognize our sin is to see ourselves as God sees us, and then to understand our human efforts to make ourselves holy is filthy rags. We must understand God will not dismiss our sins because "He understands we are only human." We must not make excuses but make confessions to God, admitting our sinful condition. Jesus is our only hope.

The Point: Our transformation continues as we learn to "hate evil" in our world, community, home, and selves.

- Why is it important to hate evil?
- How is hate a positive emotion?
- How does hating evil help your focus on loving God?
- What actions reveal to others how much you hate evil?
- What actions can you take to increase awareness of your hate of sin?

26

"Love must be sincere. Hate what is evil; cling to what is good." (Romans 12:9)

As an adventurous and invincible teenager, I would do anything! Four of my friends and I decided we would do what no man had ever done: walk across the Ohio River under the train bridge! We rode our bicycles downtown and parked them on the hill next to the tracks, where we would begin our adventure. Below the tracks was a single, two-inch by twelve-inch board used by the service crew to make inspections and repairs. Our wooden path to adventure lay before us, and we were geeked!

With much jubilation and faux fanfare, we started our journey. While walking slightly hunched over and ducking under crossbeams every four or five steps, we bravely traveled toward our ultimate goal: Ohio! We laughed, joked, and spoke greatly exaggerated words of our courage and status as community heroes. Everything went as planned as we traveled about a quarter mile, fifty yards beyond the West Virginia side of the river. Then we felt something strange in our feet and legs: vibrations!

A slow-moving coal train entered the bridge where our journey began, and we had no escape plan. Someone yelled, "Grab a beam!" So we did. At first I used only my hands, but as the train came closer, I hugged the beam so tightly I think I left indentions in it. When the train was above us, I held my head back as far as I could so my face would not bounce off the beam. Being too manly to scream and afraid I would wet my pants, I held on for dear life. Someone yelled, "Everyone okay?" but his voice vibrated so badly we could not understand.

An eternity later (about five minutes), the train passed, and none of fell the seventy-five feet into the river or wet our pants. We silently walked back to our starting point. We'd had all the adventure we could handle.

Webster's Online Dictionary defines *cling* as:

> 1 a: to hold together
>   b: to adhere as if glued firmly
>   c: to hold or hold on tightly or tenaciously
> 2 a: to have a strong emotional attachment or dependence

Webster perfectly defines my relationship with the beam, as well as what my relationship with God's truth must be. I have failed here too often.

The first step to revealing our sincere love to a lost and dying world is to "Hate what is evil, and cling to what is good." Let's put the definition in today's verse.

The Point: "Take action against evil. Hold together; adhere as if glued firmly to; hold tightly or tenaciously to; have strong emotional attachment to or dependence upon what is good."

- How does being transformed by the renewing of your mind apply here?
- By applying this principle, how does your daily walk with God look?
- On a scale of 1–10, how do you rate your "cling to what is good" efforts?
- What actions can you take right now to "cling to what is good"?

✎ How can you explain this new understanding to your men's group?

Slow down! Allow time for this to expand your theological comfort zone!

27

"Be devoted ..." (Romans 12:10)

I like sports, but I am not very good at any of them. Don't take me wrong; I wanted to be the star player on each team. I simply did not want to practice. I tried baseball, basketball, football, and track. No matter what the scenario, the result was the same: I did not make the team. I was not devoted to any sport, and so developing the disciplines and skills necessary was too much work and not enough fun.

Then I discovered bowling. Some say it's a game and not a sport. Whatever it is, I'll leave it to the experts to define. I liked bowling so well that I purchased a ball, bag, towel, glove, shoes, and rosin bag. My wife and I joined two bowling leagues and regularly practiced to hone our skills. I talked about, read about, practiced, and lived bowling. It was always on my mind, and I paid the price to participate. I was devoted!

In Webster's Online Dictionary, I discovered that in order to understand *devoted*, I had to understand *devotion*. Below are the two definitions.

> Devoted: characterized by loyalty and devotion
>
> Devotion: 1 a: religious fervor: piety
> 2 b: the fact or state of being ardently dedicated and loyal

Men tend to be loners and gravitate to our garages, our man caves, the forest, or bodies of water. We say, "I like being by myself after being around people all day. I don't like crowds. I need some peace and quiet." And here is the kicker: "I like just me and God hanging out together." That sounds real holy and pious, doesn't it? Although these contain a thread of truth, usually the driving motive is that men tend to be loners.

Many men I know are devoted to their families, for which I am thankful. Their devotion is biblical, necessary, and an enormous blessing as men flesh out their love for their families. To an Alpha Male, this is the first item on their priority list!

Being devoted implies we open our lives and invite other men into our world. We resist being lone wolves, and we interface with other men as we actively share real-life experiences so that each person will grow in his faith walk with God. It's messy work, but worth the effort.

The Point: The intensity of our devotion determines the level of our loyalty.

- What drives you to invite other men into your life?
- What price do you pay to hone your "be devoted" skills?
- How have you given your undiluted loyalty to men who need Christ?
- To whom do you flesh out "the fact or state of being ardently dedicated and loyal"?

28

"Be devoted to one another …"
(Romans 12:10)

Years ago, I was confronted with a situation that had the potential to ruin our organization's reputation for decades. A person sat before me in tears and told me of an elected board member violating a moral law. This failure will damage any organization, however for a small organization in a rural community in the Bible Belt, the blow was most devastating.

The timing for this news was worse. I was in the throes of a series of important meetings and had to leave in two hours for that evening's meeting. I knew I could not wait until next week to respond. With a broken heart, my wife, Susan, asked a simple question: "When [not "If"] will you confront this?" She knew delay was not an option.

"Right now." I replied as I walked out the door. Knocking on her door was the hardest thing I ever did. Her body language revealed nervousness. and our discussion was tensely quiet and cautiously direct. Twenty minutes later. she resigned. and I left with a broken heart. pleading for God's grace and mercy on all of us.

Two weeks later, the gossip explosion happened, and fallout blanketed our community. A couple months later, I was told we victoriously overcame the scandal because I'd confronted the situation before it became community news. I did not feel like I victoriously overcame the scandal. I felt like I'd barely survived.

In the New Testament, we are admonished to "___ one another" over fifty times. The sheer number of occurrences demands we investigate this precept, making it part of our God walk hiking gear.

This "one another" phase means we man up and do what must be done for the sake of others. We catch the ball, take the hit, make the sacrifice, and risk the loss, all for the sake of others. "One another" reveals to me it is always about God and others and never about me. Many understand this, but Alpha Males do it.

Confronting the situation held up God's standard of holiness of heart and life, offered her the opportunity to repent and confess her sin, and protected innocent others from blame and criticism. I launched into action because of my devotion to the guilty parties, their families, my organization, and our Lord.

Bob, now deceased, was a journeyman welder. He told me his final test for certification was welding two pieces of steel together. After welding them, a steel rod was placed under the full length of the weld, and a press pushed down on the parallel edges to bend it at the weld. If the weld broke, he failed. Bob passed. He said, "You can only test the weld when it's under pressure. Any weld will hold when it has no stress."

The Point: The level of our devotion to one another is tested when we are under pressure to do what is best for one another.

- How has your devotion to one another been tested?
- If you passed the test, what attitudes, behaviors, and choices helped?
- If you failed, what could you have done differently to pass?
- List a few questions you have so that you may ask other men their thoughts.

Intermission

Take a deep breath, hold it for three seconds, and exhale. Ah! Feel better? Repeat as necessary.

The introduction states,

> Our journey to Alpha Manhood is difficult, and so few take it. Many want the easy route, and so they accept the world's definition of an Alpha Man and build a façade, concealing their true identity. They take the wrong trail, the external trail.
>
> The internal trail to true Alpha Manhood is revealed in Scripture. Only men who deeply desire Alpha Manhood take this journey. As in mountain climbing, only those who possess the do-or-die mentality reach the summit. They discover the reward is greater than their dreams, and they gain benefits that cannot be fully expressed in earthly language

Reading this intermission reveals you are tough and determined because you have not quit. Way to go! Alpha Manhood is becoming your lifestyle!

The principles you learn are direct, clear, pointed, and purposeful. The illustrations are personal, revealing, and as transparent as I can be right now. I trust you are encouraged and challenged to improve your faith walk with the Lord.

I know this journey is tough, and your self-preservation instinct may have kicked into high gear. However, I also know growth only happens when we accept the challenge to stretch, grow, and become completely uncomfortable. There are no La-Z-Boy recliners on the path to growth!

Just before my father retired, he asked personnel how many retirement checks the average retiree received before he died. He was stunned when they said, "Eight, because they retire to their favorite chair and the TV remote control." In other words, they retire to nothing. *Retire* means "to take out of service; to be rendered useless and have no value."

Many men retire from the hard work of personal, spiritual growth, and service. They want the easy life they think they deserve. Without intentional effort, they unknowingly drift backward. I hear much too often, "I've served my time," suggesting serving the Lord is similar to a prison sentence!

Alpha Males refuse to retire from discipleship. To reach the summit, they intentionally keep climbing. Alpha Males know climbing upward to success is their only option. Will you continue to climb?

- What is your proof you have not spiritually retired from discipleship? From personal and spiritual growth?
- Will you live until you die, or will you quit living and wait to die?
- Why can't we relax and enjoy the trip?
- List benefits from your intentional effort toward Alpha Manhood.
- Challenge: Find the word *retire* or the concept in your Bible.

29

"Be devoted to one another in brotherly love …"
(Romans 12:10)

No matter how you view it, there is nothing like family. Nothing is as great or as dysfunctional. The family is where we learn basic life and relational skills. We cannot choose our family, however we choose what family dynamics rule our household.

In Scripture, the Godly family is the best context to understand God's relationship with man. The interrelational dynamics of training and discipline perfectly illustrated this relationship. The Bible includes both the awful and the awesome: Some families hated, raped, and murdered each other. Other families loved, protected, and sacrificed for each other. Some openly hated God, and some gloriously loved God. One thing I love about the Bible is every deed, whether good or bad, is written in the same sized font! Whether beautiful or ugly, the all truth is presented with equal emphasis and honesty.

Within the context of family, Paul said, "Be devoted to one another in brotherly love." *Storge* means family love, and it's used only once in the Bible (Romans 12:10).

It is easier for me to love someone who does not have a lot of baggage. I know a lot of men who have multiple levels of success, and I enjoy speaking and hanging out with them. They are smart, articulate, and confident, possessing positive attitudes toward life. These guys are easy to be devoted to with *storge*.

Then there's Phil (false name). Phil is a drug addict and lost everything because of it—family, home, job, and health. He is in and out of sobriety as he battles his addiction and justifies falling back into the old habit by saying, "That's why they call it an addiction."

I counter with, "That's why the Bible offers deliverance."

Every time I see him, I ask how he is doing, and his answer is always the same: "Great!" I want to be devoted to him in *storge*, but it is hard for me. Sometimes I do not know if I am talking to the man or a drug flowing through his veins.

This I know: I need brotherly love toward Phil no matter how much his life is messed up. It is easy to love guys on top of their game. However, the true test of my *storge* is when I offer it to someone whose life is in the toilet, spiraling downward and out of control. Remember what my welder friend Bob told me: "You can only test the weld when it is under pressure. Any weld will hold if it is not under stress." Our devotion must pass the stress test!

Success is magnetic, and failure is repulsive. My prayer is not to express *storge* toward Phil, but the *storge* I express is genuine to the core. Concerning the Phils in His day, Jesus said, "I tell you the truth, whatever you did for one of the least of these brothers of mine, you did for me" (Matthew 25:40; read verses 31–46 to know the flow).

The Point: Phil needs my *storge*. I need my *storge* to be genuine to my core.

- Identify the Phils who come into contact with your life.
- If you were someone's Phil, how would you want Christian men to respond to you?
- List what you can do to express *storge* toward your Phil.
- What results do you think you will experience with your Phil?
- How can you communicate this truth to your men's group?

30

"Honor one another above yourselves." (Romans 12:10)

National Grandparents Day (the first Sunday after Labor Day) was approaching, and so we decided to honor Bruce and Mary for their lifelong service to the Lord and for being charter members of our church. Their son confiscated their address book so we could send invitations to all their family and friends. We informed our congregation about our Grandparents Day celebration and provided invitations for friends and family to this beautiful day. Everyone knew the secret except Bruce and Mary. We decorated the church with children's Grandparent Day artwork, used grandparent-friendly music, and gave each grandparent a twelve-inch-tall oak tree to plant as a family tree. I suggested they take photos of their grandkids by the tree each year to watch their symbolic and real family tree grow up together.

Grandparents Day arrived, and excitement fill the air. Fifteen minutes into the service, we quietly escorted about twenty-five family members into the service. Then we immediately announced the secret. To a standing ovation, we escorted Bruce and Mary to the seats of honor on the platform. Tears, hugs, and high-fives flowed freely throughout the congregation. With devious help from Bruce and Mary's family, we prepared a photo journal DVD and presented them with a beautiful figurine to commemorate this joyous occasion. It was an incredibly blessed day. God was glorified, and the church was encouraged by the lives and devotion of Bruce and Mary. They both are now enjoying heaven while this memory warms my heart.

Bruce's love for people was highlighted when, after my father-in-law died, Bruce told my wife that since her father was gone, if she wanted, she could call him Dad. Susan hugged Bruce, cried on his shoulder, and called him Dad from that day onward.

Webster's Online Dictionary defines *honor* as:

> **a:** good name or public esteem: reputation
> **b:** a showing of usually merited respect: recognition

If one seeks to be honored, one's quest is not honorable, and everything one does is a tool to build one's ego.

Honor is gained by a selfless, lifelong devotion of encouraging, motivating, and serving others. The honoree is usually surprised and feels unworthy of the recognition. Humility is a key ingredient. Bruce and Mary expressed their surprise and unworthiness of their recognition by saying there are others who deserved this more than they.

The Point: When you honor someone above yourself, it does not devalue you or your service. It encourages and motivates all to strive to become better servants for the glory of God. After all, it is all about Him and not about us.

- In what ways have you honored someone for their devotion to others?
- Who do you think deserves to be honored for their lifelong service?
- When would be a good time to honor this person, and how?
- Who can help you honor the person you identified?

31

"Never be lacking in zeal …" (Romans 12:11)

"I refuse to travel through life flat-footed! I refuse to carry a doom-and-gloom attitude, even when the road is treacherous and challenging. When I have days with more clouds than Sonshine; more stress than rest; more mud than meadow, I am victorious! Since Life IS Stressful,. I use my R⁴ Rule: Realize Reality - Respond Resiliently." Rev. Charles A. Bledsoe

How can we bounce back quickly? By choosing to believe God's Word! Remember, you are transformed by the renewing of your mind. By allowing the Holy Spirit to change how and what you think, you experience a transformed attitude and lifestyle by faith. Faith thoughts become faith ideas, which spawn faith actions.

Today's verse says, "Never be lacking in zeal," meaning it is our choice to lack zeal or not. It is up to us to choose to live with zeal on the faith side of life!

I'm not talking about "Fake it till you make it." We obey God until we believe Him. We choose the path paved with God's promises.

Mark 9:14–28 tells of a boy with an evil spirit. His father brings him to the disciples, and they could not heal him. Jesus told the father to bring the boy to him and then said, "Everything is possible for him who believes."

The father immediately exclaimed,

"I do believe! Help me overcome my unbelief!" (Mark 9:24).

It seems like dear old Dad spoke a contradictory statement, doesn't it? However, he said, "My heart believes but my head does not. Please help me overcome the part that does not believe!" Human logic says words cannot heal. It takes medicine and years of therapy. Sound waves moving through the air cannot heal. But faith words do!

Jesus healed the boy because the dad chose faith action instead of his head's denial. His action led his faith! This is raw, unrefined, unfinished, undisciplined, unreasonable faith. His action said, "I can do all things through Christ who strengthens me, even if my head says it cannot be done." Actions move us forward even when our head steers us toward denial and retreat.

When we chose to act in faith before we believe in faith, then our actions lead our faith until our faith grows enough to lead our actions.

Everyone has an "I believe. Help me overcome my unbelief!" moment, challenging the very core of our faith. Some overcame by faith, and some floundered in unbelief.

The Point: Zeal is raw energy generated by our faith in God's Word, a positive attitude, and our trembling, faithful action steps!

- Talk about a time when your actions led your faith.
- Discuss when your lack of faith prevented action.
- What were the consequences of both scenarios?
- How does action apply to "Love must be sincere"?
- What action will lead your men's group to step up and accomplish something big for God?

32

"Never be lacking in zeal but keep your spiritual fervor ..." (Romans 12:11)

I was the Prime Time (senior adult) ministry director for my district when the Lord gave a vision to organize a prime-timer specific work and witness (missions) adventure to Brazil. I received encouragement from our district Sunday school council, and so I uneasily launched into this very exciting first-time ministry.

Energy oozed from every facet of my life. I lived, breathed, dreamed, talked, prayed, and researched what it would take to make this vision a reality. I was pumped! We needed 20 Prime-Timers from across the United States and Canada, and so I invested about 30 hours on the Internet gathering over 1,500 e-mail address of Nazarene churches, districts, and Prime-Timers.

When a pastor friend said he would not have taken the time to gather all those e-mail addresses I Immediately remembered what Zig Ziglar wrote: "Successful people do what unsuccessful people refuse to do."

My faith-filled actions drove us to successfully recruiting twenty-four Prime-Timers for our denomination's first Prime Time–specific international work and witness mission adventure!

So how is this action any different from what is taught by the self-help gurus of this world? Simple: the world's gurus teach your success is based entirely upon you, your strength, your intelligence, and your determination. However, our success is based on God and the promises in His Word. Paul reveals this in Philippians 4:13.

"I can do all things through Christ which strengthens me."

God can do *all things* in and through our lives. This understanding creates a passion within, compelling us to action. It expresses itself through our personality, honoring and glorifying God. Passion empowers us to sacrifice, do the work, knock on the door, pray without ceasing, share our story, surf the Internet, catch the ball, study His Word, and do whatever action is needed to get the job done.

In Revelation 3:7–11, God rewards the passion displayed by the church in Philadelphia.

> I know your deeds. See, I have placed before you an open door that no one can shut. I know you have little strength, yet you have kept my word and have not denied my Name …Hold on to what you have, so that no one will take your crown.

The Point: With passion, the cost is never too high, the sacrifice is never too great, and the reward is never too low.

- How are you strong enough to remain foolish and weak?
- What doors has God opened that you have or +have not entered?
- How can you hold on to your spiritual fervor?
- How can you help others gain or keep their spiritual fervor?

33

> "Never be lacking in zeal but keep your spiritual fervor serving the Lord." (Romans 12:11)

I'm stuck! What can I say about serving the Lord that's not already been said? What personal illustration can I download to enlighten and challenge you to step up to the plate and swing for the fence? God never fails. However, words do, and I am in a linguistic tar pit. Where is Ernest Hemmingway when I need him?

Serving the Lord is the result of keeping our zeal and spiritual fervor. If the Lord is not the subject of our zeal and spiritual fervor, then we are basically a "resounding gong or a clanging cymbal" (1 Corinthians 13:1). We merely sing praise to secular humanism because it is all about us and our accomplishments. Feel free to take a bow while facing the mirror; the person you see is your greatest fan, worthy of your finest praise!

As a young teen, I mowed lawns. One client asked me to cut her grass shorter. I said my mower was set as low as it could go, at her request. I also said if I cut the lawn any lower, the hot sun would destroy it. She was not happy and claimed all I wanted was to cut her lawn more times than necessary to make more money. It can be very difficult to prove intent or motive. With all my zeal, I reminded her of how dependable I had been, and my fee had not changed even when gas jumped 16 percent from 25 cents to 29 cents per gallon. I also reminded her I swept her sidewalk and driveway at no additional charge. She sheepishly allowed me to mow her lawn for the rest of the season at our agreed price.

What questions can clarify your motives? It's hard for me to admit when my motives are selfish and not Christ-centered. If my motive is troubling, it is easier for me to quit looking at the motive than to change it. I'd rather not see my selfish motive than prayerfully deal with it. Pruning is painful.

I discovered when a brother in Christ questions my motive, I must carefully consider his questions and observations. One powerful benefit gained from our men's group is others see us more clearly and objectively than we see ourselves, and some will ask the hard questions. I painfully discover compassionless questions from some men can be very insightful and difficult to answer. While defending myself, I sometimes discover my true motive, and sometimes what I discover is pretty ugly.

The Point: We do not have to convince God our motives are pure; He already knows the truth. The challenge is to face the truth and ask God to transform our motives.

- What are you doing to keep your spiritual fervor?
- How are you expressing your fervor?
- Whom can you partner with so both of you will express spiritual fervor?
- When will you ask him to be your accountability partner?

34

"Be joyful ..." (Romans 12:12)

Legend says Sam Lord built his castle from wealth gained by looting ships. He placed lanterns in trees and built fires on the beach, in a small cove with shallow water covering a high coral reef just outside of Bridgetown, the capital city of Barbados. Passing ships were lured into the cove by the fires, thinking they were at Bridgetown. Once the ship crashed onto the reef, his men would row out to loot and burn them. He was highly successful at creating confusion. Today his castle is a hotel at the same private cove.

Confusion is when something has various components that cannot be differentiated. The definitions below, from Webster's Online Dictionary, really don't help clear the fog surrounding our understanding the difference between joy and happiness.

Joy

> **a:** the emotion evoked by well-being, success, or good fortune or by the prospect of possessing what one desires: delight

Happiness

> *1:* good fortune: prosperity
> **2 a:** a state of well-being and contentment: joy
>   **b:** a pleasurable or satisfying experience

The saying "Happiness comes from happenings, and joy comes from Jesus" gives a little glimpse of the difference between the two, with joy having all the power.

Hebrews 12:2 states, "Jesus …who for the joy set before him endured the cross, scorning its shame." Jesus endures scorn and shame because of joy, not happiness!

James 1:2 says, "Consider it pure joy, my brothers, whenever you face trials of many kinds." Joy is what Jesus used when He faced the cross, and it is what we need when we face trials of many kinds. Not happiness but joy.

Joy is based on Jesus Christ. Joy enables us to look beyond our present circumstance and see our ultimate glorification. Jesus looked beyond the pain and suffering of the cross, beyond the scorn and shame of dying like a criminal, to receiving the absolute fulfillment of God's promise by being seated by the right hand of God and providing us with salvation!

The absolute fulfillment of God's promise is not to endure and be victorious on earth but to spend forever with Him. If we only see earthly victory, we are short-sighted. We must see eternal victory as well. Too many men are consumed with trying to be successful in this life they do not faithfully seek Christ for the life to come.

The Point: Joy comes as we focus on Jesus and not a comfortable now.

- How can joy empower you to endure the trials of life?
- What does seeing beyond earthly trials to you being in heaven do for you?
- How does this spawn a hurricane of joy in your heart and mind?
- How can you express joy in your daily walk with your Lord?

35

"Be joyful in hope …" (Romans 12:12)

Twins have their own dreams, ideas, and plans for the future. Yet many parents cannot think about one without thinking about the other. Even though each twin is an individual, they are forever conjoined in the minds of their parents. The same is true about joy and hope. One cannot exist without the other because they share a single heart!

Many mistakenly equate hope and wish as the same. Wish is dependent upon luck, the universe aligning in a certain order, winning some sort of cosmic lottery, or other people doing things accidentally to fuel their fortune. A wish is whimsical, a puff of smoke, a cloud of steam.

Hope is a desire with an expectation of fulfillment. Hope is based on the person and deity of Jesus Christ. In 1834, hymn writer, C. Michael Hawn, declared, "My hope is built on nothing less than Jesus blood, His righteousness.…" Hope comes from accepting Christ as our savior, and is rooted in God and His promises, which are as dependable and eternal as God Himself!

A wish has no moral boundaries; for example, a man may feel lucky because a coworker is receptive to his sexual advances.

Hope has moral boundaries, because hope is rooted in Christ Jesus. Romans 6:1–2 says, "Shall we go on sinning so that grace may increase? By no means! We died to sin; how can we live in it any longer?"

Hope removes our quest for luck and elevates our dependency on providence. Providence is based on God's will and plan for our life. Hope transcends this earthly life and empowers us to see our eternal existence! First Corinthians 15:19 says,

> "If only for this life we have hope in Christ, we are to be pitied more than all men."

Hope is not a product of this world because it comes from God and finds its fulfillment in eternity with Christ. When we reduce hope to a single day's allotment, we discover joy. When we extrapolate joy over a man's lifetime, we have hope. Hope sees beyond the things we gather around us in this life and looks beyond the grave and into eternity with God. Hope enables a positive attitude toward life and the awareness of a glorious future in eternity.

Faith brings joy, and joy spawns hope. Hope cannot exist without joy any more than joy can exist without personal faith in Jesus Christ.

The Point: Joy provides energy for today's sprint. Hope provides endurance for life's marathon.

- ✏ State your understanding of what "be joyful in hope" means to you.
- ✏ In your opinion, what is the power packed in this verse?
- ✏ How can this change your attitude and approach to faith and life?
- ✏ Discuss a time when hope worked in your life.

36

"Be joyful in hope, patient …" (Romans 12:12)

I'm a computer speed junkie. Most men are. When we buy a new computer, we want the fastest processor known to man and the most RAM possible so we can cyber-travel at the head of the pack. I crave cyber-speed! I want it all, and I want it yesterday!

In our instant-gratification society we hate to wait. We want our own perpetual go-to-the-head-of-the-line card for every event. We are like drivers who inch forward at traffic signals until they are past the line where they should stop.

First Corinthians 13:4 says, "Love is patient." The first quality for love is patience.

Webster's Online Dictionary defines patient as:

> **1**: bearing pains or trials calmly or without complaint
> **2**: manifesting forbearance under provocation or strain
> **3**: not hasty or impetuous (acting out of emotion and not thought)
> **4**: steadfast despite opposition, difficulty, or adversity

The definitions apply to difficult times in life and not good times. Waiting means to stand still, expecting to receive something you desire. A patient Alpha Male does not get angry.

Let's apply these definitions.

When life gives pain and trials, remain calm and do not complain; stay the course. When being provoked or stretched to your limit, manifest restraint, not anger. When you need to advance and others stand in the way, do not act carelessly, thoughtlessly, forcefully, or violently. When opposed, confronted with difficulty, or treated adversely, stay steadfast, and firmly fixed, and unmovable in the Lord.

Alpha Males should:

- Stay faithful to their calling because they know God will deliver.
- Deal with the shortcomings of others without becoming angry.
- Advance in spite of others.
- Not act thoughtlessly or violently.
- Remain unmovable when opposed by evil forces.

The Point: Waiting is like the hundred-meter sprinter in the starting blocks: tense. Patience is like the marathon runner catching his stride and relaxing.

- What are the differences between waiting and patience?
- What do these definitions teach us about the other?
- Because patience is not a product of this world, how can we attain it?
- What benefits does patience add to your life and testimony?
- Who needs to learn this truth from you?

37

"Be joyful in hope, patient in affliction …" (Romans 12:12)

Wham! It felt like I had been hit in the back with a baseball bat. I bent sideways, and my leg pulled up because it would not stay on the floor. I experienced difficulty breathing and felt nauseous while the room spun. I was frozen to the dresser. My wife began to fire off a series of fear-generated questions I could not speak to answer. "What's wrong?" she asked a half dozen times.

I finally squeaked out, "Kidney stone." Previous experiences taught me this painful truth. My patience was nonexistent, and I was in immediate, unimaginable pain. I have also discovered emotional and professional afflictions can be just as unexpected and painful.

"We want you to change your ministry focus," is how I received the news my four-year, successful ministry now belonged to someone else.

"I don't want to change ministry focus. I really enjoy what I am doing," I replied.

"That position is no longer yours," my superior (not the decision maker) said. "Take this new assignment so I will not lose you from our district council."

Because I was no longer the director of that ministry, I lost my seat on the denominational council as well. I suffered a double whammy over which I had zero input or control. Four unreturned phone calls and six unanswered e-mails to the decision maker left me feeling betrayed, hurt, and frozen in time.

Webster's Online Dictionary defines affliction as the state of being in pain or distress. *No one* wants pain. Affliction in our life is as guaranteed as sunrise each morning. God never promises us life is fair; He only promises His grace is sufficient. Whether the affliction is self-generated or at the will of another, the hurt is just as painful, and the council in this verse is the same.

The definitions for patience reveal how our obedient response strengthens our testimony and glorifies our Lord. Job loss, outsourcing, corporate greed, financial reverses, rebellious children, and physical illness require we reexamine these principles to shore up our testimony and honor the heavenly Father.

Alpha Males know patience is a "Fruit of the Spirit," as discussed in Galatians 5:22–23. You can try using your own strength to stay calm, or you can allow the Holy Spirit to work His patience through you. Choose wisely.

The Point: Affliction is promised. Grace is guaranteed!

- What does Galatians 5:22–23 teach you about patience?
- How can affliction build your faith and build your life?
- What can you learn about yourself from how you handle affliction?
- How can you teach this principle to your children or grandchildren?

Note to self: Thinking is hard work. Don't cop out!

38

"Be joyful in hope, patient in affliction, faithful ..."
(Romans 12:12)

There I was, twenty-five feet above the ground and standing on a twenty-inch square platform, strapped in a safety harness with a line fastened to a cable above my head. I was about to walk thirty feet across a one-inch cable to another platform. To say I was scared is an understatement. As I delayed my journey, the instructor yelled, "Have faith in the safety equipment! Trust the harness!" This new experience was well outside my comfort zone. From the ground it looked easy, however I gained a new perspective while standing on the platform. I took a deep breath, nervously put my foot on the cable, and told God to hang on to me as I took my first high ropes course journey

"Have faith in the safety equipment!" echoes in my mind even today and comes to the surface when I face a challenge bigger than me. I don't mean a challenge I can organize and plan my own path through, but a challenge requiring I trust the safety equipment because I am destined to fail without it. To succeed at life, we need faith in God's safety equipment.

Once again, you must view faith as a verb and not a noun. As a noun, faith is simply mental gymnastics, intellectually agreeing to what God says is true. As a verb, it propels you into action and transforms your behaviors into action steps dependent upon God to make them successful. Anyone can build a good men's ministry in his mind, but only those who convert their thoughts into actions will do so. To win the game, you must get off the bench and put your thoughts and prayers into action! Many talk, but few take the journey.

Faithful does not mean being full of thoughts that agree with God's truth. Faithful means doing what God commands. Faith is physical proof God is able to do abundantly more than we can ask or think! James, Jesus's half brother, addresses this concept in James 2:14–26. See this in verses 17–18, 20, 26.

> In the same way, faith by itself, if it is not accompanied by action, is dead. But Someone will say, "You have faith; I have deeds." Show me your faith without deeds, and I will show you my faith by what I do … You foolish man, do you want evidence that faith without deeds is useless? … As the body without the spirit is dead, so faith without deeds is dead.

Alpha Man-Up and read verses 14–26. It is vital you know the flow!

The Point: God's Word is our safety equipment. Read it! Trust it! Obey it!

- Discuss a time when your walk did not reach the level of your talk.
- How can an action-based faith transform your life?
- How will this affect your daily journey with God?
- Name an action step to start your faith-based action plan of faithfulness.
- Whom will you team up with to build your faith-based action plan

39

"Be joyful in hope, patient in affliction, faithful in prayer." (Romans 12:12)

"We have to talk" are four words I hate to hear my wife say, because I know I am in trouble—again! Even when reduced to "Let's talk," I still have a sinking feeling in the pit of my stomach. It's classical conditioning, by Susan, the best behaviorist I know. Whatever the case and no matter how creative she says this, I still want to crawl into my man cave and hide.

Many men feel the same way about prayer. We would rather hide and ignore than speak to our Lord. Why? Do we do really believe God is there, or that He listens to us or answers our prayers? Or does our DNA make us so logical we grasp only the concrete and shy away from faith-based conceptions? Maybe we think prayer is not good time management.

Whatever the basis for our prayer-less lives, we must find the catalyst to ignite this vital spiritual discipline. We seek to be "transformed by the renewing of our minds" so that we engage in activities allowing us to willfully, intentionally, and personally speak with God. In *Primal: A Quest for the Lost Soul of Christianity*, Mark Batterson writes,

> So many people struggle with cultivating a prayer habit simply because they don't know what to say. Their prayers consist of overused and misapplied Christian clichés. Or they feel that prayer is a one-way

monologue. The truth is, the Bible is God's way of initiating a conversation with us. And it turns prayer into a dialogue. God talks to us via Scripture, then we talk back.

For me, Mark's statement is spot-on! Reading the Bible is the first action step we can take as we cultivate a prayer life. In my personal experience, I've discovered that no Bible reading equals no prayer life. What about you?

"I don't like to read," you say. I have three words of unimaginable power for you: Get over it! If reading is difficult, then get a Bible on CDs or cassette tapes (do they still make cassette tapes?), or download it to your phone. Listen in your car or while doing chores. The point is you must interface with God by engaging Him with His primary method of speaking to you. Once you learn to hear His voice through the written Word, you will be able to hear His "still, small voice" when he speaks deeply to your heart, where no one else can hear but you.

The Point: Pick up your Bible and listen!

- Why do you think it is important to read your Bible?
- What is your best, daily scheduled reading time?
- What do you have to do to read through your Bible once each year?
- To whom are you accountable for maintaining a prayer discipline?
- When will you call him to discuss your accountability and ask his help?
- How can you teach other men the benefits of Bible reading and prayer?

40

Okay, Time to Stretch!

Lean back in your chair, stretch your legs as far in front of you as possible, and then stretch a little farther. Point your toes forward while at the same time reaching as far over your head as you can. Hold this for a few seconds and then exhale and relax. Repeat as necessary.

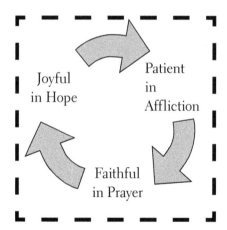

This feeding-cycle graphic illustrates the characteristics learned in the previous six pages. Each is nourished by the one before and feeds the one that follows—biblical codependency at its best!

- In your opinion, which one is the most important? Why?
- How do the others support the one you selected as most important?
- By removing one, what happens to the others?

- How does this interconnectivity build strength in the believer?
- List one spiritual goal you will accomplish this week with God's help.
- Now list the first step you must take to reach that goal.
- When will you take the first step?
- To whom will you be accountable for taking the first step?

41

"Share ..." (Romans 12:13)

"Share with your brother and sister." "It's good to share." "Don't be selfish." These are admonitions my mother used to encourage me to practice daily.

Our understanding of the verb *share* is giving to others out of our abundance. This makes us feel good and blesses the one receiving. Anyone with abundance can do this because it has little effect on the bottom line. However, Jesus taught us to give even when we are in need ourselves.

> He also saw a poor widow put in two very small copper coins. "I tell you the truth," He said, "this poor widow has put in more than all the others. All these people gave their gifts out of their wealth; but she out of her poverty put in all she had to live on." (Luke 21:2–4 NIV)

Jesus teaches when we give out of our poverty, we bless God. Can you close your eyes, see the expression on His face, and hear Him speaking this verse as He witnesses her sacrificial gift given from her own deep need?

I know men who are talented tradesmen and professionals. These men gladly use their life skills as a ministry to help those who cannot afford these services. However, some will not share their greatest gift: their testimony. They gladly give God praise with their hands but not their voices. We must do both.

No matter how limited our earthly resources, we all have an overabundance of spiritual resources. We can never deplete the resources God is pouring into our lives. His supply is infinitely greater than our storage capacity. As soon as we give a bushel away, God refills us. We never operate with a less than a full supply.

Our greatest earthly needs are shelter, food, clothing, and someone to love and listen to us. People's greatest spiritual need is the saving grace of our Lord Jesus Christ. Help someone with their earthly needs and have the courage to share God's love for them through your personal story, telling them what God does in your life. Focus on telling God's story in your life and then follow the Holy Spirit's leadership for encouraging them to accept Christ as their savior.

The point: The only thing you have in abundance is God's grace. Share it!

Here a guide to organizing your story.

1. **Make it personal.** It's about your walk with God.
2. **Make it current.** It's about what God did in your life during the last couple of weeks.
3. **Make it glorify God.** Give Him all the credit.

Write your story following this three-step guide with a two-minute time limit.

42

"Share with God's people who are in need ..." (Romans 12:13)

I love mission adventures! I organized eleven and led nine mission teams, and joined a team to Cuba from my local church. We traveled to Toronto, Brazil, Barbados (four times), Jamaica (four times), and Cuba. If you want your heart stirred, your thoughts challenged, and your local church globalized, then join a mission team! Your devotion to the Lord will grow more in two weeks than listening to a year of sermons and bible studies because you are investing your heart and life in others. You will never see your church, your world, or your life the same way again.

You will no longer be a local church Christian. You become a world Christian with a global view of the Church that Jesus Christ died to save, purify, and empower. Christian mission adventures make Matthew 28:18–20 a personal challenge and a present-day reality.

Everywhere we travel, the local people share what little they have with us and I feel convicted because the person annual income is one-tenth or less than mine. How can I accept a gift from his very limited supply when his basic needs are not being met? How can he who has so little give so much to me, who has so much and gives so little to others? Read 1 Kings 17:1-16.

I tend to give from my abundance and not from my heart. When presented a need, I use a system to determine whether I will support this need and what level is comfortable.

1) Do I want to support this need? Does this need move me?
2. I examine my budget to see how much financial wiggle room I have.
3) When I find my "comfort limit," I decide whether I want to give all I can or just part of it.
4) What if another need is presented, and I use all my wiggle-room money for this need?

What do we discover when we research the word *share* in the original biblical language? We discover *share* does not take into consideration what the giver does or does not have. This command does not apply only to those who have more than they need, or applies only if our family budget has wiggle room. We discover the command is based on the other person's need and not our abundance or wiggle-room ability to offer support.

The Point: The command to share is not based on the giver's excess or wiggle-room. The command to share is based on the recipient's unmet need.

- How do I determine what I give, and to whom?
- What sharing lessons are taught in 1 Kings 17:1-17?
- What do these lessons encourage me to do?
- Other than giving money, what other sharing can I do?
- How do I allow God to transform my thoughts and actions, improving my share-ability?
- How does sharing demonstrate "Love must be sincere" in Romans12:9?
- What prevents me from sharing?

43

"Share with God's people who are in need. Practice …"
(Romans 12:13)

"Practice makes perfect" irritates me because I do not want to practice. I want to be perfect without all the work. Where is the app to instantly transport me to perfection? Practice is hard work and takes too long. I want it now, without a plan or pain!

Instant gratification is the heart cry of many, resulting in self-centeredness. Many can name prominent people who flesh out this ugly craving for immediate gratification at all costs.

Truthfully, practice does make perfect. Thomas Edison was asked how it felt to fail so many times as he tried to invent the incandescent light bulb. His response illustrates the need to persist in practice:

"I have not failed. I've just found 10,000 ways that won't work."

John Cooper, former head football coach at The Ohio State University, made a statement from which I devised these formulas.

$$\text{Practice} + \text{Time} = \text{Skill}$$
$$\text{Skill} + \text{Opportunity} = \text{Success}$$

Every man wants to be successful to avoid failure, so we stubbornly stick to what's in our comfort zones. Spare time is in short supply, and so we reluctantly carve out time for anything unless our return on investment is worth our time, money, and effort. This is called consumerism—an enemy of spiritual growth.

Malcolm Gladwell, a bestselling author and journalist, claims the "10,000-Hour Rule" is the key to success in any field. It's a matter of practicing a specific task for ten thousand hours to develop the necessary skills to become an expert. Ten hours per week times fifty weeks equals a twenty-year journey! Success requires long-range grit and painful self-discipline. Success isn't cheap!

Shortcuts are risky and littered with broken lives and dreams. They do not allow time to develop skills in order to sustain our gains or adequately prepare us for future challenges.

The Point: Shortcuts short out our potential and short-circuits our future. Practice well! Practice long! Practice intentionally! Don't give up!

- How can you carve out the time needed to grow your spiritual life?
- How can you build your stamina and determination to not quit?
- How does your belief in God's promises impact your ability to succeed?
- What does "You perform at the level you practice" teach you?

44

"Share with God's people who are in need. Practice hospitality." (Romans 12:13)

"Charles Allan! Is that any way to treat your guest?" When mom used my middle name, I knew I was in dire straits. She wanted me to be nice, whatever that meant. Although I had a stubborn tendency to refuse to fit into a box created for me by others, I realized Mom was right. How we treat our guest is vitally important.

> Hospitality is being kind and receptive in welcoming strangers and guests to our gatherings. We only have one chance to make a good first impression, so we should take advantage of our one and only first shot. Let's put the definition into Paul's command: "Practice being kind and receptive when welcoming strangers or guests."

It's easy to welcome friends, however Paul is concerned about how we welcome outsiders. It takes practice to not sound professionally polite or mechanically friendly when we welcome strangers. By viewing nouns as verbs, we define what hospitality looks like to the strangers we welcome into our group. Read Romans 12:14–21 because Paul is teaching us how to welcome the enemies of Christ into our Alpha Men's group. Do you agree? Why or why not?

Some are uncomfortable around men they do not know, and even more so with those they fear or do not like. Because Paul is an evangelist, his heart throbs to win the lost to Christ. He wants us to warmly welcome those needing the Savior no matter what lifestyle they live. Our calling is to be the open door to the open door. We need a "transformed mind" to become "kind and receptive when welcoming strangers and enemies." Let's practice.

Here are a few simple questions I use as I greet strangers at our church.

- "Hi, I'm Charles." I extend my hand. "I'm glad you're here!"
- "Is this your first time here?"
- "Do you live around here, or are you visiting the area?"
- "Is there someone here you came to meet?"
    - If yes, I help them find their friend. If no, I become their friend.
    - I immediately introduce them to those standing nearby and offer them a cup of coffee.

The Point: How we welcome strangers must reflect how Christ welcomes us.

- How do you approach first-time visitors to your church or men's group?
- What simple questions do you ask visitors in order to gently engage them?
- Describe your first experience as a stranger at a church. How did the greeter make you feel?
- What does a sincere welcome look like to the visitor?
- Describe how you will greet a stranger this week.

45

"Bless those who persecute you; bless and do not curse." (Romans 12:14)

The contrast in this verse is easy to see. However, when we read it in light of "practice hospitality," we may not understand how deep this river runs. Our corrupted human nature tells us we must not do this. This verse cuts through religious talk and confronts our God walk.

From my experience, all spiritual endeavors and belief systems that are not based on a personal relationship with Jesus Christ are nothing more than legalism—man's efforts to save himself through intellectualism and self-discipline. Alpha males do not want an exterior change only; we want a new heart that changes what others see in us. We want our exteriors to be true to the Holy Spirit's empowered transformation.

Dictionary.com defines *bless* as a verb. Three definitions clarify how we bless our guests.

1. Request God bestows divine favor on them.
2. Bestow good of any kind upon them.
3. Protect or guard them from evil.

> In contrast, Dictionary.com defines *curse* as a verb. The <u>expression</u> of a wish that misfortune, evil, doom, etc., befall a person, group, etc.

Let's put these definitions in the today's verse.

Request God bestow divine favor upon your guests as you bestow any kind of good and protection from evil upon them. Do not express a wish for misfortune, evil, or doom to befall them.

Alpha Males realize this level of acceptance is impossible using human strength. While Christ hung on the cross, He said, "Father, forgive them for they do not know what they are doing." Jesus welcomed His enemies to the cross so His blood would pay for their redemption. He asked God to bestow divine favor upon them and to not let misfortune, evil, or doom befall them. On the cross, He sought salvation for those who were crucifying Him! Our call is to be Christ-like.

The Point: Sincere acceptance of God's enemies into our fellowship can only spring forth from a heart transformed by the Holy Spirit.

- What must I ask God to do in me so I may accept/bless others?
- What spiritual disciplines help me continue my transformation?
- What enemy can I approach and welcome into our fellowship?
- How does the absence of a blessing default into a curse?

46

"Rejoice with those who rejoice, and mourn with those who mourn." (Romans 12:15)

Polar opposites! From the mountaintop of extreme joy to the abyss of extreme sorrow, this verse bookends the wide range of emotions we men experience. It is a clear revelation we must identify with each other across a massive range of roller-coaster emotions. Of the two extremes, I'd rather celebrate with a brother, wouldn't you?

Celebration is fun! Roaring laughter, high-fives, leaping chest bumps, powerful bear hugs, and mountain man handshakes are ways we men express ourselves in our celebration rituals. Grins stretch from ear-to-ear, eyes explode with light, voices are energized by excitement, and joy flows from the hearts of men celebrating God's blessings bestowed upon a brother! "Rejoice with those who rejoice" is your invitation to the end-zone celebration, the NASCAR winner's circle, or the Olympic medal platform. Don't miss the party!

Mourning is not fun. Slumped shoulders, bowed heads, painful isolation, screaming silence, and festering buried emotions are ways we men express our mourning rituals. With solemn faces, dull eyes, and low voices, sadness oozes from our hearts as we seek solitude and isolation. "Mourn with those who mourn" is our invitation into a very difficult abyss with a brother's suffering: pink slip downsizing, a doctor's tough news, divorce paper delivery, or a daughter's heart-wrenching announcement. You do not want to miss being "Jesus with skin" for a brother in need.

It takes an Alpha Male to descend into the abyss with a suffering brother. What makes it so difficult? Sometimes fear hinders us—fear of not knowing what to say or do, fear of how your brother will accept you, fear because you may secretly be in a similar situation.

Sometimes it is jealousy or envy stopping us from celebrating. It may be pride or arrogance. All these are sin and must be confessed to the Father as we give Him permission to transform us into flawed men of faith.

The Point: Fear, jealousy, or envy will hinder our walk with our brothers in Good times or bad. Don't make excuses—make prayers. Celebrate or mourn with your brother.

- What was it like the last time you celebrated with a brother?
- What was it like to descend into the abyss with a brother?
- What will you ask God when you pray about your transformation?
- When will you share your thoughts with your accountability partner?
- Confess this weakness to your Lord right now.

47

"Live …" (Romans 12:16)

Every Saturday morning, my elementary age self would plop down in front of our TV and watch three hours of cartoons. Every Saturday morning, my mother would say, "Quit wasting your life in front of the TV. Go outside and play with your friends. Do something worthwhile!"

Alpha Men intentionally live. They demand their lives count for something worthwhile. They strive to be productive, to contribute to the wellbeing of society, and to aspire for their world to be a better place. Alpha Males choose to make a difference.

Paul says, "Live." Do more than occupy time and real estate. Don't spend your life—invest it! Don't burn time—redeem it! Don't piddle or meander aimlessly; focus on a worthwhile goal, vision, or dream and relentlessly pursue it with redemptive passion and determination. Do not retire (to take out of service or make obsolete) but reenlist. Choose to live beyond breathing, eating, and having a heartbeat. Determine to allow the Holy Spirit to fill your heart, pulsate through your veins, and empower you to live a holy life, Alpha Male style!

By your example, teach others how to purposefully live the Gospel with words.

> Preach the word; be prepared in season and out of season; correct, rebuke and encourage-with great patience and careful instruction. (2 Timothy 4:2 NIV)

This verse can easily become, "Tell your story; be prepared." You can also teach others without words.

> Let your light shine before others so that they may see your good deeds and glorify your Father in heaven. (Matthew 5:16 NIV)

This can easily become, "Live intentionally before others."

The Point: Dominate life with intentionality, purpose, vision, and passion. Make your life benefit others and glorify God. Embrace Paul's life purpose recorded in Philippians 1:21. Be fully alive in Christ!

- How are you living your Alpha Male life with intentionality? With purpose? With vision? With passion?
- How can your life benefit others and glorify God?
- What must you become to quit existing and to really live?
- How can you explain the principle of living to your teenager?
- How will you explain this principle to a male friend who really needs to hear this truth? When will you discuss this with him?

48

"Live in harmony with one another." (Romans 12:16)

Remember the 1971 Coca-Cola jingle, "I'd like to teach the world to sing in perfect harmony"? Okay, quit singing and keep your day job!

I love male-quartet, four-part harmony. A soaring tenor tickles the clouds. The deep bass lays down the foundation. The mid-range voices tie it all together into an amazing sound of perfected talent. In my opinion, no group does it better than the Gaither Vocal Band. (I know they have five members.) If only I could sing like David Phelps!

What does "live in harmony" look like? It is a life complementing community life. Just as the body is one with many parts, the Church is one with many parts. Living in harmony is when each person contributes to the total well-being of the entire community by coordinating one's efforts with the effort of others.

We are blessed to live in the United States, the greatest county in world. We are still called the Great Experiment because we have the first government of its kind in history. Our constitution guarantees the rights of the individual, and these rights are vigorously defended. However, the demand for individual rights has a negative effect when it is brought into the Church.

> Acts 2:1 records the final command Jesus gives to His followers: "Do not leave Jerusalem, but wait for the gift my Father promised."

His followers stayed in Jerusalem, and ten days later, "when the day of Pentecost came, they were all together in one place." "All together" means they were united by one mind and one purpose, with each sacrificing their rights to experience a corporate blessing for the common good of all.

We must not demand personal rights or privileges because to be united in Christ means we deny ourselves, take up our cross, and follow Him. We desire to fulfill God's purpose in order to reach all men with the good news!

Unity in essentials and tolerance in nonessentials is our theme. Demanding personal rights or preferences divides the Church and destroys our witness. The opposite of demanding our rights is discovering and developing our spiritual gifts. This is our only hope to unite the Church and position us to receive God's blessings and strength in order to reach our neighbors for Christ.

The Point: Selfless living creates harmony. Individuals contribute what they do best so the Church can fire on all cylinders, fulfilling the Great Commission. Harmony attracts; disharmony repels!

- How can I quit demanding my rights and live in harmony?
- What should I ask God as I pray He helps me with this issue?
- How can we explain this concept to men who do not serve Christ?

49

"Live in harmony with one another. Do not be proud …" (Romans 12:16)

"Take pride in yourself. Don't be too proud. Be proud of your work. No one likes a braggart. Take pride in your appearance. Don't be arrogant." Mom sure knew how to confuse a skinny kid with low self-esteem. Many of us live in the same overpopulated state of confusion concerning pride and arrogance (P/A) versus pride and confidence (P/C).

What can we expect when we cross the border between good and bad pride? Here are a few observations from being on the wrong side of this war many times.

P/A closes doors to relationships. A haughty spirit offends. When P/A is the product of real success, others feel this attitude as a slap in the face of their success (or lack thereof). Arrogance repels and builds walls, and so the person with P/A lives in a world of one. Like the old Three Dog Night song says, "One is the loneliest number that you'll ever do."

P/A stops learning. Proverbs 27:17 says, "As iron sharpens iron, so one person sharpens another." From others, we learn attitudes, alternative methods, skills, vision, goals, determination, motivation, creativity, ways of God, faith, humility, gratitude, and many other things. If we separate ourselves from other men, all this stops, changing Proverbs 27:17 to say: "as iron standing alone becomes dull, so one man standing alone is dull."

P/A stops teamwork. Shelves of books are available concerning teamwork, so read one. The reality of increased success through teamwork is well documented. Eleven men, each doing a specific assignment, will enable the entire team to score even through only one man carries the football across the goal line. Teamwork is uniting skills and purpose wrapped in trust and interdependence to reach a common goal. P/A closes this door and decreases your success ratio and altitude.

It's interesting to note Paul's encouragement to "Live in harmony with each other" is followed by "Do not be proud." P/C must also be true. P/C coupled with humility opens doors to relationships, learning, and teamwork. I heard a speaker say, "Nothing of any spiritual significance happens outside of a good personal relationship." P/C opens doors; presents opportunities to learn, and builds teams. Relationship building is hard, messy work, but so is landscaping. However, after landscaping is done, the end result is amazing!

The Point: Alpha Men learn from each other the value and benefits of serving God as a team.

- How open are you to relationships, learning, and teamwork?
- How do you hinder building relationships, learning, and teamwork?
- Why is Jesus's humility so magnetic to you?
- How can you become magnetic to those who need Christ?

50

"Live in harmony with one another. Do not be proud."
(Romans 12:16)

So how does confidence look when fleshed out in the life of an Alpha Male? What are the benefits of confidence?

P/C draws others into your presence. People want to be in the presence of a confident man who has more wins than losses. However, the Christian Alpha Man does not seek self-glorification. As you read the biographies of successful Godly men, a common thread is that they did not set out to become famous. Many started their journey wanting to be faithful to God's calling and leadership in their lives. As they became successful in the eyes of the world, many embraced the attitude that their success is a means to provide opportunities to help others become successful. This attitude is extremely powerful in drawing others into the vision of the successful man.

P/C is ever learning. Confident men realize everything can be improved. I love Honda's advertising that says, "Better is a never-ending quest." Confidence allows the Alpha Man to realize he does not know it all, and it empowers him to listen to others and learn from them no matter how successful they are. Great men have a hunger for greater knowledge in their field of expertise and beyond.

In Philippians 1:12, Paul writes, "And this is my prayer that your love may abound more and more in knowledge and depth of insight." It's interesting to note *abundance* is a noun and *abound* is a verb! So what action do you see when an Alpha Man's love "abounds more and more in knowledge and depth of insight?? Note that "more" is addition, whereas "more and more" is multiplication!

P/C promotes and grows teamwork. As confidence oozes from an Alpha Man, men desiring to be Alpha Males join his team. Teamwork must be cultivated and experienced by all. Pat Riley, former coach to the world champion LA Lakers, said when the ball goes through the hoop, it takes ten hands to put it there. Coach Riley lived, breathed, taught, and demanded teamwork from his players. When everyone helps everyone else, everyone wins! Arrogance drives men apart; teamwork draws men together. No one wants to play with a ball hog!

The Point: Alpha Men who draw men into their influence, are ever learning, and build teams so that everyone wins the championship ring!

- What guards the boundary between arrogance and confidence?
- Describe your team-building efforts and attitudes.
- What steps do you need to take to improve your team-building skills?

Where else can you learn more about team building than with your band of brothers?

51

"But be willing to associate with people of low position." (Romans 12:16)

"This is my friend, Jaun," Bill said. "Would you mind if he hangs with you while I play in the praise band?"

Juan was a nineteen-year-old visitor at our church, and so I introduced him to a two other men standing nearby. Juan has a difficult time initiating a conversation with strangers, and I'm exactly the opposite. My dad said I can talk to a fence post.

Every gathering, whether comprised of humans or wild beasts, has a hierarchy (stated or unstated). We rank people by money, looks, occupation, education, possessions, combat skills, class, and more. Today's verse recognizes this and deals with the attitude that must prevail throughout the entire brotherhood.

To you, what is the most important word in this verse? Why?

To me, it's *willing*—to exercise the power to choose without being coerced, manipulated, or forced. *Willing* is genuine and honest, has trustworthy intent and motive, and is not reluctant, hesitant, or motivated for personal gain. *Willing* is a decision that says, "I choose to invite, greet, and welcome your without hesitation and with genuine humility."

Paul challenges our motive, not our behavior, because behavior always conforms to motives. Can a leopard change his spots? No, because a leopard's external self is true to his internal self. God does not want behavior modification but heart transformation that changes behavior. God wants our external selves to be true to our internal selves—genuine to the bone!

How we treat other men makes an eternal difference in their lives and relationship with Christ. Through my pastoral years, I learned people wanted three things from the church: to be accepted for who they are and not for what they can contribute; to be loved unconditionally and without reservation; and to be comforted, like connecting with old friends and family. A simple way to begin this journey with an associate is to sit with him during the gathering, introduce him to several other men present (especially the pastor and group leaders), serve him coffee and treats, and give him a calendar of upcoming events. No training necessary—just a willing servant's heart.

A friend of mine has a humble servant's heart. He reveals Jesus to everyone because of his willingness to serve anyone in any way he can. He is genuine to the bone, and so for me he is a good example. I thank God because he's my friend.

The Point: Your willingness gives God permission to do in and thru you anything He desires so men can come to know Christ.

- How do you rate your servant's heart on a scale of 1–10?
- How do you associate with or serve others who are of low position?
- For what will you pray to become a better servant?

52

"Do not repay anyone evil for evil …" (Romans 12:17)

"He hit me first!" was my defensive justification. As a kid, I misunderstood the "eye for an eye" in a non-Christian way. I took complete advantage of every situation by repaying the offender with principle and interest.

Paul understood and knew crossing this bridge made the next crossing much easier and the journey into this forbidden land much deeper. He knew the addiction of retaliation became stronger and more severe every time it was used, and the way out became longer and more difficult.

This is a command and warning. First, this command protects the believer's witness. Satan is very subtle as he cloaks his evil intent with the façade of biblical justice. He knows if we repay evil with evil, our desire to extend justice intensifies as we teach the offender to not mess with God's man, or else he will face our righteous indignation. This attitude is produced by a mind conformed to the realm of the unredeemed.

Paul knows the problem in the Roman church. He understands this attitude and behavior will destroy the church and cripple their witness, making the Gospel a big joke in the eyes of the unsaved. Left unchecked, the disastrous ramifications are extensive, intensive, and expensive!

The only revelation unsaved men see is the lives we live. They cannot see the Holy Spirit filling our hearts or empowering our will. They can only see what we do and say, and they feel the attitude we project. These three things comprise our witness, and the power of our witness is our transformed minds firmly rooted in God's truth and energized by Christ living in our hearts.

Second, our obedience reveals God's love and forgiveness offered to the offender. Men may think we are great guys, kind, compassionate, and fair. However, it's not about us; never has been and never will be. It's about God working through us to reach those who do not have a relationship with Creator. Our obedience is the only Gospel rebels read, so print clearly!

The Holy Spirit empowers us to return good for evil. Our behavior is so contrary to what men usually see that they are caught off guard, surprised, stunned, and maybe even confused. Whether or not they question our response, one thing is for sure: they know we are different, and that's exactly the image God wants them to see!

The Point: Evidence of a transformed mind is the fleshing out of mercy, grace, forgiveness, and hope to men who have none.

- Describe the last time you crossed the bridge to retaliation.
- Describe the last time you revealed to the offender the love of Christ.
- What does God have to do in you to improve your witness?
- Ask Him to do it right now. Remember, if not now, when?

53

"Do not repay anyone evil for evil. Be ..." (Romans 12:17)

I remember my early encounter with the verb *be*. I was thoroughly confused how *be* becomes *am, is, are, was, were, be, being,* and *been*. To say it's an irregular verb is an understatement! Recently I began taking a CD-based Spanish language course, and in lesson three I realized we were conjugating the verb *be* again. I had enough trouble in English! However, no matter how much trauma this interjects into my life, *be* is important to understand and properly use.

The verb *be* is not a behavior. It is a transforming lifestyle, it's becoming, not just doing. If a man behaves like a warrior and then is confronted with a real in-your-face challenge, he had better be a warrior to the core, or else he will painfully discover the difference between external theory and internal reality.

The warrior does not just act like a warrior—he *is* a warrior from his very core to the tip of his fingers. As a lad, David revealed his Alpha Manhood when he confronted and defeated Goliath. Goliath's fatal mistake was he only saw a shepherd boy and not a warrior king!

David became a warrior by his absolute faith in God's indwelling presence for the strength and ability to victoriously defeat any challenge. Our willingness to develop total confidence in God's indwelling presence makes us victorious against all challenges and is incredibly important to understand and apply as we strive to become alpha males.

Outward appearance is misleading. It's inward toughness that drives an alpha male to continue in spite of the obstacle, pain, or challenge barricading his path to success. Completing the task, objective, or goal is what is important. The barricade is not as important as our response to the challenge set before us. Do we whine and complain about the difficulty. Trust the Lord to give you the wisdom, insight, and power to overcome everything blocking your way.

> "If God be for us, who can stand against us?" (Romans 8:31)

You see, it is not about us. It never has been and never will be.

The Point: Inward transformation is not man-made but God-created within us. He is empowering us with His Holy Spirit so we become more than conquerors in Christ.

- What experiences confirm your trust in God's indwelling presence, which empowers you to overcome obstacles blocking your path to success?
- How can we have faith in God's promises to become like King David?
- What can you do to help men become Alpha males?
- What goal requires you to trust God more now than you ever have?
- If money, time, and talent are unlimited, what will you do for the Lord?
- What do you think is the first step toward that goal?
- What do you think are the next three steps?
- When is a good time for you to take the first step?
- Who can encourage and motivate you to do so?

54

"Do not repay anyone evil for evil. Be careful …"
(Romans 12:17)

"Be careful" is a universal admonition given by parents to their children, especially when they are driving. Mom said it to me as much as I say it to my daughters. I'm sure the same is true for you and your kids.

"Be quiet" means you become noiseless. "Be encouraged" means you become courageous. "Be careful" means you become alert to danger and avoid unnecessary, high-risk behaviors. However, it does not mean to not take risks. Some have become careful yet climb mountains; surf enormous waves, and enter very dangerous anti-Christian places to preach the Gospel and make disciples, knowing any of these adventures could cost them their lives. Dr. John slipped into Red China a couple of nights a month for about four years to help an underground church make Christlike disciple. He willingly risked his life to fulfill the Great Commission. All of these individuals became careful, yet their definition of *careful* covers a lot of risky territories.

A former co-worker of mine did not just talk about being a special forces member—he became one. One story concerns the time it was his turn to jump out of an airplane without a parachute, trusting his teammates to catch him before he hit the ground. He jumped, and they caught him. Why did he take this crazy risk? Because he had been part of the catch team several times, and his experience empowered him to trust his team. When you know the One you trust will catch you, you may ignore the risk, and leaps of faith become common. God's redemptive work continues! The only way to know God will catch you is to jump!

I teach an adult class where we discussed *faith* and *believe*" as verbs and not nouns. Someone said, "We do not believe what we know." That statement caused me think about many "They do not know what they believe" and "They do not know what to believe" moments. It's no wonder men sit quietly in the pews and do nothing. We are taught that *faith* and *belief* are nouns requiring no action. Acting upon what you believe changes a mental exercise into an action-filled, exciting, transformed, risk-taking lifestyle.

In his book *No More Christian Nice Guys*, author Paul Coughlin addresses the weakness in the modern Church because men are spiritually soft and lack strong masculine leadership, and the freedom to take God-ordained risks. These are needed to drive the church toward God-ordained risk-taking adventures such as going into the world and making Christlike disciples. Coughlin's book is a must-read for men who wish to become an Alpha Males.

The Point: *Be* is a verb that points us toward transformation!

- What does *be* mean to you concerning your Christian faith?
- What mental belief are you acting on with physical behaviors?
- What is God pointing you to become?
- Whom will you phone today to discuss this thought?

55

"Do not repay anyone evil for evil. Be careful to do what is right." (Romans 12:17)

As we admonish our kids to be careful, we are encouraging them to make decisions to act in ways proven to be safe and wise. When driving, it means: keep a safe distance from the vehicle in front of you; do not use your phone; wear your seatbelt; at night, do not overdrive your headlights; and dozens of other safety tips. In other words, do what is right and what is proven to be safe.

Take two seconds to reread the verse above. Notice the contrast. How can you paraphrase this for your sixteen-year-old daughter? I agree that it's tough to do. Why? Because human nature demands we do unto others as they do unto us! It's exactly opposite to the Golden Rule, "Do unto others as you would have them do unto you." Maybe this is our reasoning for returning evil for evil to those who mistreat us.

"Be careful" is a yellow caution flag demanding our attention and obedience. It's an invitation to stop in our tracks, take a deep breath, reconsider our options, and then choose the best path to travel. Every NASCAR car driver knows what the yellow flag means, and the wise heed its warning.

I'm reminded of a story about a smaller high school kid who was an easy target for bullying and general harassment. One day he came home from school unusually upset. After some fatherly prodding, he finally told his dad about a much larger boy making his life miserable. His father asked, "Can anything be done to stop the bullying?"

After some discussion, the son said, "I know! I'll become his friend. I'll invite him to church and ask him to stay over on Saturday night. We can rent a movie and play some Wii games." His dad agreed the idea was worth pursuing.

The next day, the boy went to the bully and asked if he wanted to come over on Saturday and play some Wii games, spend the night, and go to church with him on Sunday. The bully was stunned! He asked, "Why would you want me to be your friend? I have been so cruel to you."

"Because that is what Jesus wants me to do," the boy answered. The bully accepted the invitation, and his bullying immediately stopped.

The Point: Consider the negative attention someone gives you as their need for you to "be careful to do what is right" concerning them. Maybe Jesus is leading them to a careful you.

- Discuss how ugly behavior is a bully's way of calling out for your friendship?
- Discuss how the Holy Spirit leads bullies to you and for what purpose.
- How can you take advantage of God sending you a mission opportunity?
- What is the first step you take to "be careful to do what is right"?
- Name someone with whom you must "be careful to do what is right."

56

"Be careful to do what is right in the eyes of everyone."
(Romans 12:17)

What's a guy to do when he does what is right and faces criticism? All of us who strive to do the right thing and later have our motives questioned know exactly how it feels. We also know what it is like when we question the very truth upon which we based our actions. We know the gut-wrenching turmoil we endure when we ask ourselves, "Was it worth it?" or, "Why did I get involved?" We may even take a severe, defensive posture and decide to make "Live and let live" our motto, knowing this is very selfish and uncaring. So what's an Alpha Male to do, especially in light of today's Scripture?

Every time this verse comes up in Bible study, I hear the same objection: "It does not mean we are doormats!"

When I ask, "What does it mean to you?" all I get are blank stares or faces looking downward. We know what it does not mean, however we need to know what it *does* mean. Notice the contrast between the first part of this sentence and the second. "Be careful" introduces the rest of this principle. It is important we do not separate this into two disconnected thoughts because each clarifies the other.

It does not mean to permit the unpredictable wind of public opinion to determine what we do, say, or think. It doesn't mean we conform our behavior to what others say we should or should not be doing. It does not mean abandoning our will, or what we know is right, to accept the will of others as our own. List a few other things we sense this does not mean.

"What is right in the eyes of everyone" does not mean we are to do what others say is right. Jesus said in Luke 16:15, "You are the ones who justify yourselves in the eyes of others, but God knows your hearts …" I suggest "in the eyes of everyone" means we do what is right so that all men can see with their own eyes what is right. This keeps our witness pure and true to God's Word. By doing this, our doing right is in the eyes of everyone.

Men know right from wrong. Many oppose, resist, and ignore the truth so that they can keep doing what they like doing. When we "Be careful to do what is right," and men see our actions with their own eyes, they see the truth. And that, my friend, is very powerful and penetrates the hardest of hearts, pricking the conscience and planting a seed for God to reap. Our eyes are our strongest receptors; a picture is truly worth ten thousand words. The unsaved hang pictures of what you do on the walls of their memory.

The Point: Talk is cheap and easy. Action is clear and powerful.

- How does "What you do speaks so loudly that I cannot hear what you say" (Ralph Waldo Emerson) affect your understanding of this verse?
- How does this affect your behavior and witness?
- How do others interpret your testimony if it does not match your lifestyle?
- Name men with whom you can discuss and explain this new thought.

57

"If it is possible° "(Romans 12:18)

"You can do anything you want to do. What the mind can conceive it can achieve." Dozens of other motivational statements continue to challenge us to think bigger, reach farther, work harder, and believe stronger. Even the Bible addresses this issue:

> "I can do all things through Christ who gives
> me strength" (Philippians 4:13).

If all these statements are true, why does Paul write "*if* it is possible"?

As a child, when I cooperated with my parents, my life was much easier. This was highlighted by the many times I refused to obey. My parents could not make me obey, however they could make me wish I had obeyed. My disobedience taught me valuable lessons and made me count the cost of my decisions.

These same lessons apply to my discipleship with Christ. I've learned the terrible defeats of choosing to ignore God's leadership. I have also experienced amazing blessings as I choose to cooperate with God and follow His leadership. Ignoring God's leadership is always costly. Obeying God's leadership is an investment in Him paying future dividends well beyond anything I can image.

The bottom line is that God created humans with a free will. Humans are free to determine their thoughts, attitudes, actions, behaviors, and future. They're free to accept or defy God's will, salvation, and transformation. They are free to choose their life path with full awareness of eternal consequences. Joshua said, "Choose for yourselves this day whom you will serve, but as for me and my house, we will serve the Lord" (Joshua 24:15); read the entire chapter for more context.

God is a gentleman and will not overpower your right to choose. However, He does reveal His will, and He encourages us to choose His path. We are free moral agents, not puppets dancing on the end of spiritual cords manipulated by the almighty marionettist.

What about us? Why do we resist, ignore, and defy God's leadership? Why do we continue to think our ways are better than God's ways? This resistance proves our need to be transformed by the renewing of our minds. Transformation is painful. Only men who truly crave to be Alpha Males push through the pain and climb to the summit. Please know the higher we climb, the greater the pain because Satan does not give up. He knows we seek comfort and ease over discipline and growth. Prove your possibility—keep climbing!

The Point: Your cooperation with God's Word removes *if* in today's verse.

- How has your obedience to God's Word affected your life?
- How has your disobedience to God's Word affected your life?
- Describe some spiritual growing pains you have experienced.
- Explain how you successfully climbed over tough places.
- Discuss what you want your life to be in five, ten, and twenty-five years from now.

58

"If it is possible, as far as it depends on you …"
(Romans 12:18)

"Do your part" is the admonition my parents gave us when we siblings were given large cooperative chores like cleaning the yard. My usual response was, "But what if Ray or Cheryl won't do their part?"

"Do *your* part!" was the usual reply. I would spin around and begrudgingly start the chore, grumbling beneath my breath with anger and exaggerated movements. As an adult, I have learned to hide this attitude by not having exaggerated movements, however the internal question of "What if° ?" is still the same.

Remember that the context of this verse is showing hospitality toward an enemy who is attending our men's group. This verse assumes the enemy is not inclined to give us the same grace and courtesy we extend to him. If he is not doing his part to promote peace, we are not permitted to forgo our promotion to a peaceful settlement.

"As far as it depends on you" places biblical responsibility upon both parties. However, this is aimed directly at the Alpha Male seeking transformation. You're right: it isn't fair. However, being "careful to do what is right in the eyes of everyone" protects our witness to the transforming power of Christ.

"As far as it depends on you" releases us from being accountable for the other person's response to the olive branch we offer. As the old saying goes, "It takes two to tango." By accepting responsibility for our part, we change the dance.

As our daughters found themselves in relationship struggles, I said: "Don't feed the fire." I was a former volunteer fireman and learned that in order to put out a fire, we must remove one or more of three things: heat, air, or fuel. By refusing to discuss the situation with friends; by refusing to say confrontational, cruel, or critical things to or about the other party; and by being cordial to the other party while sincerely asking God to help, I remove heat and fuel so the fire will go out. I have personally discovered it is hard to hate someone for whom I am praying. As I pray for an enemy, I sense compassion for him building up within me. It's strange ...or is it?

The Point: Do your part and trust God to do His. Stop dancing to the wrong music!

- Does this devotional make sense? Why or why not?
- How can knowing how to put out a fire help you with tough relationships?
- Name someone with whom you need to put out a fire.
- What is the first step you must take to begin putting out the fire?
- What would be your second and third step?
- When will you take your first step?

59

"If it is possible, as far as it depends on you, live." (Romans 12:18)

"You only live once. Don't waste your life. Do something great." These are statements I've heard for as long as I can remember. Most of the time, they washed over my head without going into my ears. It was not because I had a hearing problem but because I had an attitude problem. God's solution is personal transformation.

What does *live* mean? Once again, to know what it means, we discover what it does not mean—comparison/contrast teaching at work again.

> *Live* does not mean to breathe, eat, drink, move, work, play, or reproduce. Many people do these yet do not have a life. Jesus said, "I am come that they might have life, and that they might have *it* more abundantly" (John 10:10).

Does this mean Jesus came so that we may breathe, eat, drink, move, work, play, and reproduce more abundantly? We're talking about Godly quality and not humanistic quantity of life.

Live smacks of intentionality, purpose, personal growth, progress, fulfillment, significance, service, legacy, and much more. Alpha Males want to live, take risks, conquer, climb, overcome, invent, excel, move mountains, explore, discover, build, create, teach, and hundreds of other verbs! We would rather our lives be like the white-water rapids of the Lochsa River in Idaho than the boringly smooth running Ohio River in the Midwest.

The word intentionality sums up God's will for our lives. He wants us to be intentional, not accidental or serendipitous. We should wade into life on purpose and with a purpose, with eyes open to the pros and cons yet wading in anyway. Alpha males may consider wrestling a running chainsaw if the challenge intrigues us enough. When asked why he climbed Mount Everest, Englishman George Mallory said, "Because it's there." They are the three most famous words in mountaineering.

With courage, we approach other men with the intent of winning them to Christ. Why? "Because they're there." We can accept a difficult or dangerous challenge because He's there. We approach God with a prayer for transformation "Because He's there." I heard a senior adult say he wanted to live his life like driving a sports car. When his time is up, he wants to race into the cemetery, and while sliding sideways toward his grave, he'll lean out the window and shout, "What a life!" In other words, he wants to intentionally live with excitement and risk until the end!

The Point: Choose to intentionally live! Don't quit living years before the end of your life!

- What does intentionality look like to you?
- What will it take for you to live till the end?
- List things you can change to make your motto "Live intentionally!"
- How does this change your attitude toward growth and evangelism?

60

> "If it is possible, as far as it depends on you, live at peace with everyone." (Romans 12:18)

Our family's car trips included potential back-seat wars because my brother sat on the right, my sister was in the middle, and I sat on the left. Being seated fairly comfortably did not exclude potential tension and tough attitudes. We used the pattern in the seat fabric to designate boundary lines. Heaven help the trespasser who inadvertently invaded the other's domain. Mom frequently asked, "Why can't you just sit there and be quiet until we get to Grandma's house?" That was easy for her to say because she was not in the back with her two siblings for the forty-five-minute drive. Dad's comment was always, "Don't make me stop the car!"

We all know people who make relationships difficult. So how does this verse guide us? The phrase "at peace" seems to say peace is a destination, like "at the beach." In my little brain, this phase is different from "in peace" just like "at water" is different from "in water." I am trying to understand what Paul is saying, so your thoughts are welcomed!

If "at peace" is a destination, then it implies we intentionally direct difficult relationships toward peace by continually offering an olive branch.

The olive branch has many expressions: encouragement, uplifting, complimentary, kind words, cordial mannerisms and attitudes; thoughtful gestures, and genuine praise for a job well done or a good idea. It's also the absence of gossip, backstabbing, negative competitive spirit, and more. Remember, Paul precedes this instruction with "as much as it depends on you." Our intentional actions to move this relationship toward peace is our direct responsibility.

We are not accountable for the direction the other party is driving. We are only accountable for the direction we are driving. Galatians 6:9 is very appropriate: "Let us not become weary in doing good, for at the proper time we will reap a harvest if we do not give up."

When the olive branch is received and offered back, we know both parties have arrived at peace, and from that moment forward we live in peace. Does this make sense?

The Point: In every difficult relationship, someone must intentionally steer toward peace.

- Identify someone with whom you have a difficult relationship.
- What actions have you used to extend or remove the olive branch?
- What would you ask God if you were to pray about this relationship?
- If you were to intentionally offer an olive branch, what would the first step be?
- When will you take the first step toward peace?

61

"Do not take revenge, my dear friends ..." (Romans 12:19)

We've seen it dozens of times. Football player A gives a cheap shot to player B, who gives it right back. The yellow flag is thrown, and player B is penalized for unsportsmanlike conduct while player A gloats back to his team. The one who retaliates gets penalized while the aggressor gets off scot-free. How fair is that? The best defense against revenge is found in Romans 12:17: "do not repay evil for evil."

Paul told Alpha Males ("my dear friends"), "Do not repay evil for evil," because God hates evil. If a Christian repays evil for evil, God will throw two yellow flags. Both are held accountable for doing evil to each other, and both are penalized. However, the greatest loss is the immediate damage to the Christian's witness because the non-Christian says, "And you call yourself a Christian!"

Everything God does is redemptive. Everything! When He destroys His enemies, it is a redemptive message to other God haters to repent. When Christians suffer at the hands of God haters, it is a message to Christians to trust God to deliver us from the hands of our persecutors. God's motives are always holy, and ours are not. That's why Paul teaches us, "Do not take revenge."

Should evildoers go free? Of course not! The difference in revenge and justice is the motive. The motive for revenge is to inflict the greatest amount of pain and suffering possible. The motive for justice is to punish the lawbreaker within the law and to redeem. The "eye for an eye" precept means the punishment should not exceed the crime. In other words, we do not cut off a boy's hand because he stole a candy bar, and we do not cut out his tongue because he lied.

I know a retired state trooper who asked several convicted, jail-bound criminals a simple question: "Was it worth it?" Every convict said no. While enduring great pain, motivated by frayed emotions and encouraged by a fallen nature, these men and women delivered personal revenge on the person who hurt their families, creating even more pain because the convicts' families were losing another member to prison.

Legal justice is allowing offenders to experience the consequences of their behaviors with the goal of rehabilitation. Properly administered justice strives to be redemptive to all and to provide closure for the offended family. Man's justice is never as pure as God's justice.

The Point: God's justice is always redemptive. Human revenge is not.

- How does revenge damage the Christian's witness and integrity?
- How does not taking revenge strengthen the our witness and integrity?
- How does revenge and justice differ?

62

"But leave room for God's wrath, for it is written: 'It is mine to avenge; I will repay,' says the Lord." (Romans: 12:19)

I had an older (authoritarian, dictatorial, bossy) brother and a younger (baby, puppy-dog-eyed, I'm-going-to-tell-Mommy manipulator) sister, making me the perfect, well-rounded, middle child. (Sorry, Ray and Cheryl. It's my story, and I'll tell it my way!) How do you think I responded when they would say, "Dad told me to tell you to …" You're right! You'll get the same reaction when you try to do God's job.

There are things God reserves for Himself that we must leave alone. For instance, we are commanded to not judge other men because this is God's job. When exercising wrath toward a lawbreaker, God says, "Do not take revenge." It's God's way of saying, "Get out of my way. I'll take care of this." But why?

God commands us to stay out of the wrath business because:

1. Our motives are not always pure and redemptive.
2. We are emotionally involved with the situation, which colors our thoughts.
3. We cannot see the big picture or the long-term effects.
4. The offender will resist our involvement and say, "Who do you think you are? I know what you have done. You're no better than I am!"

5. We will damage our witness and effectiveness with the offender, and others will think we overstepped our authority.
6. "Leave room for God's wrath" is simply "Get out of the way!" Do not interfere with God's responsibility and timing. God may throw the yellow flag against us! Get the point?
7. Our intervention says we have a better way because God is not acting quickly or severe enough.

God protects us from harm by doing the heavy lifting, and administering wrath is extreme heavy lifting! Mark 12:30–31 tells us,

> Love the Lord your God with all your heart and with all your soul and with all your mind and with all your strength. The second is this: 'Love your neighbor as yourself. There is no commandment greater than these.

The Point: God's job is to avenge the offended. Our job is to witness to the offender.

- List ways revenge is exercised other than physical violence.
- Discuss ways you saw revenge expressed toward others or yourself.
- How would you feel if someone took revenge against you?
- How would you feel if you took revenge against someone?
- What are the benefits of letting God be God in a situation like this?
- How does a transformed mind help us with this challenge?

63

"On the contrary ..." (Romans 12:20)

As a fourteen-year-old Boy Scout, I knew all the answers. Just ask me! Our troop traveled to Lake Logan State Park in southern Ohio for a ten-mile hike. Five of us decided we did not have to stick with the slowpokes and pushed ahead of the pack.

We should have been at the end of the trail by 3:00, so at 4:30 we realized we had a problem. I knocked on a farmhouse door and told the elderly couple our plight. They invited us in, gave us hot chocolate, and called the ranger's station. Forty-five minutes later, we were rescued. Our scout leaders calmly questioned us, and we realized we had turned left at a blue marker instead of right at the orange marker.

"On the contrary" is the fork in the trail where we make important decisions. Every man stands at the fork in the trail multiple times each day. Sometimes the decision is very easy, and we don't slow down. Other times we pause to contemplate and sometimes rationalize our decision. Making the right decision is not always easy. We calculate the differences by the cost. To us hikers, the cost was five extra miles on a cold, rainy, fall Saturday. In life, the cost can be much higher with devastating consequences or glorious benefits.

Every fork in the trail is important. Choose prayerfully and cautiously.

> But if serving the Lord seems undesirable to you, then choose for yourselves this day whom you will serve. (Joshua 24:15)

> We will not listen to the message you have spoken to us in the Name of the Lord. (Jeremiah 44:16)

Stop right now and read both chapters containing these quotes. Know the context.

The best time to make a life-altering decision is before you face it. Pre-decide to serve the Lord no matter what the cost. Joshua did:

> "But as for me and my house we will serve the Lord" (Joshua 24:15).

The Point: "I have decided to follow Jesus, No turning back, No turning back," is Jadon Lavik's method for being victorious before he faces life's most serious decisions. What's yours?

- ✒ Discuss a time you made the wrong decision at a fork in the trail.
- ✒ Discuss a time you made the right decision at a fork in the trail.
- ✒ What were the consequences of each?
- ✒ How can you explain this important message to your teenagers?
- ✒ Share with another man who really needs to hear this truth.
- ✒ Who do you think could be your accountability partner?

64

"If your enemy is hungry, feed him; if he is thirsty, give Him something to drink." (Romans 12:20)

"Why don't they get a job at McDonald's?" a teen girl asked as I was sharing some Third World people's struggle to feed their families. While explaining how our fundraiser would help feed ten families for a year. she spoke up again. "I thought they hated us." That country's government expressed hatred toward the United States, but the citizens did not, and they needed our help. By the way, there were no McDonalds in that country.

To properly understand this verse, it's essential to understand what precedes it.

Verse 16 says, "Live in harmony with one another."
Verse 17 states, "Do not repay anyone evil for evil." Verse 17 also says, "Be careful to do what is right in the eyes of everyone."
Verse 18 tells us, "Live at peace with everyone"
Verse 19 says, "Do not take revenge but leave room for God's wrath."

Then there's verse 20. "If your enemy is hungry, feed him; if he is thirsty, give him something to drink." What are we to do with all this?
God wants us to step back from the person wanting to deliver great harm to us, understand how God wants us to respond to our enemy, and get out of God's way so He can administrate His judgment and wrath. Then God calls us to step back into our enemy's presence and offer him whatever he needs to sustain his life and health.

Our Alpha Male transformation requires intentional effort to extend compassion toward our enemy, who hates us and is determined to wipe us from the face of the earth. It's one thing to pray for them, but it's an entirely different situation to enter into their presence, offer life-sustaining gifts, and know they may kill us the next time they see us. We may not identify with this very well, but Israel truly does.

Discover what the United States did for Germany and Japan after World War II, and for Iraq after Desert Storm.

Remember that our war is not with flesh and blood, but with powers and principalities. We must overcome the enemy by trusting the Holy Spirit to fight our battles for us and in us.

One more note: Recognize that the enemy's hunger and thirst is not a complete list of needs we are called to meet. Paul could have easily written, "If cold, give coat; if sick, give medicine; if worried, give hope; if unsaved, give the Gospel."

The Point: Because God's justice is redemptive, our calling is to offer sincere compassion to our enemies and present the Gospel to them.

- List two or three things you can do to help your enemy with a need.
- How can you apply this principle to an enemy at work?
- How would you explain this truth to teenagers and relate it to North Korea, Iran, and countries that hate the United States, Christ, and His Church?
- What can your men's group do to help a current God hater you know?
- Read Proverbs 25:21–22.

65

"In doing this, you will heap burning coals on his head." (Romans 12:20)

"Give it to your brother," Mom demanded.

I replied, "I'll give it to him, all right!"

I'm sure you understand what my mother said and what I said had opposite actions. My response increased my personal discomfort.

Gary Amirault quotes B. M. Bowen (www.dailygoodies.wordpress.com) to "heap coals of fire on his head." It's a figure of speech that does not mean exercising revenge or retribution. He reports it is customary for women to carry almost everything on the head without using their hands. If the fire went out in their home, she would take her brazier (a metal container used for cooking and to warm people) to her neighbor, asking if they could spare some hot coals so she could restart her fire. If the neighbor was generous, she would fill the brazier to the top and thus heap coals of fire upon her head.

> To feed an enemy and give him drink was like heaping the empty brazier with live coals—which meant food, warmth and almost life itself to the person or home needing it, and was the symbol of finest generosity. (B. M. Bowen, *Strange Scriptures That Perplex the Western Mind*)

"The symbol of finest generosity" is also of finest hospitality and grace. This is exactly what God does for us. He is extremely generous by bestowing upon us His perfect and holy grace to forgive our sins no matter what those sins are! Rev. David Gerber said, "God does not love us 'because'; He loves us 'regardless.'" In Luke 6:38, Jesus instructs his disciples to love their enemies and not judge:

> "Give, and it will be given to you. A good measure, pressed down, shaken together and running over, will be poured into your lap. For with the measure you use, it will be measured to you."

Read Luke 6:27–42 to understand the context. Too often we are guilty of changing the truth to fit us instead of allowing the truth to change us.

The higher we climb toward Alpha Manhood, the more difficult the climb becomes. One reason is we are trying to move the truth from theory (head knowledge) into practice (our daily walk). We purpose to live out His truth to honor God so all may see His love for them.

The Point: Surprise your enemy! Heap coals of fire upon his head!

- Why should the United States rebuild Germany and Japan after World War II?
- What difficulties do we experience when we allow truth to move from our heads to our hearts and into our daily lives?
- How do we heap coals of fire upon the heads of those who intentionally make our lives difficult?
- What benefits derive from allowing our lives to reflect God's truth?
- Explain how important your radical transformation is to you right now.

66

"Do not be overcome by evil ..." (Romans 12:21)

"Don't let your emotions get the best of you. Stay in control." These words were spoken to me by wise men as I worked to accomplish ministry goals during times of great frustration. Having what Myers-Briggs calls the ENFP personality (Extraverted Intuition with Introverted Feeling), I am blessed with enthusiasm and live in a world of possibilities. My favorite questions are "Why not!" and "What if?" The most common response to me saying, "I have an idea!" is usually, "Oh, no! What now?" If only I were king.

To paraphrase Paul, do not let evil get the best of you. "Do not let" says it's our choice and calls us to not allow evil to overcome us. How? Here are a few "count the cost" checkpoints that keep me focused on what is important.

1. Relationships damaged or lost; loss of credibility/integrity
2. Damaged witness/testimony
3. Loss of ministry/leadership ability
4. Damage to the Church's reputation in the community
5. Unimaginable long-term consequences that can only be semi discovered by asking, "What then?" or, "What's next?"

By realizing the value of not being overcome with evil, we find the resolve needed to remain faithful to our calling. We understand our spiritual war is not fought with human strength, skill, or ability. Our spiritual war must drive us to our Lord as we seek strength to honor Him with our transformed heart and life. Below are God's promises to us.

> When the enemy *shall come in* like a flood, the Spirit of the LORD shall lift up a standard against him. (Isaiah 59:19b KJV; emphasis added)

> Therefore put on the full armor of God, so that *when the day of evil comes,* you may be able to stand your ground, and after you have done everything, to stand. (Ephesians 6:13 NIV; emphasis added)

Alpha males refuse to accept defeat and fight to the end because we have transformed hearts and minds, empowered by the Holy Spirit. Our battle is not with an external enemy but the internal question of who's in charge, and so the only way to victory is transformation.

The Point: "For the battle is the Lord's." (1 Samuel 17:47 NIV)

- Describe a time when evil tried to overcome you.
- What did you do to resist evil and choose victory?
- What new understanding do today's verses give you?
- How do other men do to help you?
- When can you "put on the full armor of God"? Why or why not?

67

"Do not be overcome by evil, but overcome evil with good." (Romans 12:21)

"When someone is mean to ya'll, be nice to 'em!" the preacher shouted from the pulpit. "Kill 'em with kindness!" Once home, I did not find a rifle named Kindness in my Shooter's Bible. So much for that interpretation!

The "fight or flight" response is driven by our human nature. The option we choose depends upon our perception as to whether we believe we can or cannot win the fight. My natural response is evidence I need a transformed mind and heart.

Paul raises the standard when he wrote the following verses in Romans chapter 12:

"Hate evil—cling to good" (verse 9),
"Never lack zeal—Keep spiritual fervor" (verse 11),
"Bless—Do not curse" (verse 14),
"Live in harmony—Do not be proud" (verse 16),
"Do not repay evil with evil—Do what is right" (verse 17), and "Do not be overcome with evil—overcome evil with good" (verse 21), to name a few.

Verse 21 is the ultimate principle for how we are to treat those who mistreat us. Everything taught in verses 9–20 is summed up in today's verse.

Transformation makes is possible for us to fulfill our calling to become Alpha Males. God does not want wimpy Christians!

> I know your deeds, that you are neither cold nor hot. I wish you were either one or the other! So, because you are lukewarm—neither hot nor cold—I am about to spit you out of my mouth. (Revelation 3:15–16)

Instead, He declares,

> Those whom I love I rebuke and discipline. So be earnest, and repent. Here I am! I stand at the door and knock. If anyone hears my voice and opens the door, I will come in and eat with him, and he with me. (Revelation 3:19–20)

God's answer to wimpy Christians is Alpha Manhood through forgiveness, restoration, and transformation. The Alpha Males I know do not think they have arrived but firmly believe they must keep seeking, accepting, and growing for as long as they live.

The Point: God's amazing grace empowers us to gain the ultimate victory!

- What does Paul's compare/contrast teaching help us understand?
- Discuss a time when evil overcame you.
- What could you have done differently to not be overcome?
- Discuss a time when you overcame evil with good. What did you do?

Congratulations!
You reached the end!
Or so you think.

If you read every page, I believe you have interest in becoming an Alpha Male.

If you read every page *and* answered some of the questions, you are more serious about your Alpha Male quest.

If you read every page *and* answered all the questions, implementing some of these principles into your life, you are becoming an Alpha Male!

No matter how you got here, you are here. You deserve a gold star because you labored through my attempt to lead you into a very lofty and worthwhile growth initiative.

Spiritual growth is not accidental or automatic; it requires focus, intention, prayer, and faith in God. Our respect for His leadership, evidenced by our obedience to His Word, is honored by God. He answers our hunger and thirst for His righteousness (Matthew 5:6).

Some think if we go step by step, we can reach our goals by ourselves, meaning we do not need God. However, we can reach our goal only by totally trusting God to do His work in our hearts and lives. It's by God alone that we reach Alpha Manhood.

Catch the Ball is not a step-by-step guide. It's a line-by-line breakdown concerning how we apply His truth to our lives. This is overwhelming because we know we cannot do it. That's what Paul said when he wrote, "But when the commandment [law] came, sin sprang to life and I died" (Romans 7:9).

Paul knew he could not fully obey the law and make himself righteous. He needed Christ to save him by faith. There is not a program or system we can follow to work or earn our salvation.

I encourage you to fortify the weak places in your life by earnestly applying the truth presented and trust God to complete His transforming work our hearts.

As we sincerely invite Christ to be our personal savior, He forgives all our sins and makes us His son. We quickly learn it is impossible for us to continue our spiritual growth without applying to our lives biblical truth. The life application of truth is our real battle ground. Our hearts fight against the Holy Spirit to remain in control. Continually bending our will beneath God's will is absolutely necessary. This bending is what enables us to become Alpha Males.

The book of Romans outlines the path for continual growth as Paul leads us to deeper truth. Trust and dependence upon God brings us to total and complete salvation. The upward path Paul cuts leads to the summit. He never leads us horizontally. If we are not climbing, we are descending. Anyone can hike to the base of the mountain. Only alpha males climb to the summit.

It is very sad when Christian lifestyles are no different than the lives of non-Christians. Why do we accept this as the norm? How do you interpret the following?

> Therefore, "Come out from them and be separate, says the Lord. Touch no unclean thing, and I will receive you." (2 Corinthians 6:17)

We all know Christians who live one way on Sunday and another throughout the week. Maybe you are one of these. I hope not. Alpha Males hunger and thirst to become consistent witnesses to the unsaved so that we may lead them to Jesus.

This journey is difficult and seems unreasonable, unacceptable, and unfair. However, God's Word has not been compromised. When we compromise, we please everyone else except ourselves.

I intentionally filtered every thought through Romans 12:1. I trust this North Star provides a unmovable, rock-solid reference point, guiding my thoughts and personal journey to Alpha Manhood.

In Philippians 3:12–16, Paul offers his testimony (and mine).

> Not that I have already obtained all this, or have already arrived at my goal, but I press on to take hold of

that for which Christ Jesus took hold of me. Brothers, I do not consider myself yet to have taken hold of it. But one thing I do: Forgetting what is behind and straining toward what is ahead, I press on toward the goal to win the prize for which God has called me heavenward in Christ Jesus. All of us, then, who are mature should take such a view of things. And if on some point you think differently, that too God will make clear to you. Only let us live up to what we have already attained.

I trust you find guidance in this devotional. By trusting and depending upon His grace, your transformation is not only possible but very real. As you accept God's Holy Spirit, you will experience daily growth in grace so you let your light shine. Men may see your good works and glorify the heavenly Father.

Romans 12:1 is the command, and the rest of chapter 12 is commentary explaining what verse 1 looks like when it is fleshed out by Christian Alpha Males. However, Paul continues his commentary in chapters 13–15. This means if it's God's will, I will write second and third editions of *Catch the Ball* using chapters 13–15.

My prayer is that God will:

- Melt us with His holy presence
- Mold us into His holy image
- Fill us with His Holy Spirit
- Use us for His glory

Semper Fi, Brothers!

The following principles will be discussed in future volumes.

Catch the Ball II
Get Your Head in the Game
Release in 2019

Fourth Principle
 "Everyone must submit to the governing authorities"

Fifth Principle
 "Let no debt remain outstanding"

Catch the Ball III
Get Your Heart in the Game
Release in 2020

Sixth Principle
 "Accept him whose faith is weak"

Seventh Principle
 "We who are strong ought to bear with the failings of the weak"

Meet the Author

Rev. Charles A. Bledsoe is a retired pastor with the Church of the Nazarene. He served as Senior Pastor and/or as Assistant Pastor in churches in West Virginia, Ohio and Michigan, serving on district level councils on each.

His ministry extended to the denominational level serving three years on the PrimeTime Ministry Retreat Committee. While holding this positon, he became the catalyst to beginning the denominational ministry the Nazarene Motorcycle Fellowship, the first denominational level motorcycle ministry.

He taught several seminars on district, state and denominational level conferences.

Rev. Bledsoe married his two-year, high school sweetheart, Susan L. (Crump) Bledsoe, forty-nine years ago. They have two children, Stephanie (Tony) Bibee, and Jessica (Jason) Malecki; and four grandchildren: Chase (24), Alexis (10), Ethan (3) and Brooklyn Marie (7 months)

Catch The Ball was written as one more way for Rev. Bledsoe to spread the Good News of Jesus Christ.

To God Be All The Glory!

CPSIA information can be obtained
at www.ICGtesting.com
Printed in the USA
LVHW092318040419
613079LV00001B/25/P